PEOPLES AND CULTURES OF AFRICA

NORTH AFRICA

Edited by Peter Mitchell

CHELSEA HOUSE
PUBLISHERS
An imprint of Infobase Publishing

Chelsea House
An imprint of Infobase Publishing
132 West 31st Street
New York, NY 10001

Library of Congress Cataloging-in-Publication Data

Peoples and cultures of Africa / edited by Peter Mitchell.
    p. cm.
    "Authors, Amy-Jane Beer ... [et al.]"—T.p. verso.
    Includes bibliographical references and index.

    Set ISBN 0-8160-6260-9 (acid-free paper)

Nations & Personalities of Africa ISBN 0-8160-6266-8
Peoples and Cultures of Southern Africa ISBN 0-8160-6265-X
Peoples and Cultures of Central Africa ISBN 0-8160-6264-1
Peoples and Cultures of East Africa ISBN 0-8160-6263-3
Peoples and Cultures of West Africa ISBN 0-8160-6262-5
Peoples and Cultures of North Africa ISBN 0-8160-6261-7

    1. Africa—Civilization. 2. Ethnology—Africa. I. Beer, Amy-Jane. II. Mitchell, Peter, 1962-
    DT14.P46 2006
    960—dc22

                                        2006040011

Chelsea House books are available at special discounts when purchased in bulk quantities for businesses, associations, institutions, or sales promotions. Please call our Special Sales Department in New York at (212) 967-8800 or (800) 322-8755.

You can find Chelsea House on the World Wide Web at
http://www.chelseahouse.com

Printed and bound in China

10 9 8 7 6 5 4 3 2 1

For The Brown Reference Group plc.
Project Editor: Graham Bateman
Editors: Peter Lewis, Virginia Carter
Cartographers: Darren Awuah, Mark Walker
Designers: Steve McCurdy, Martin Anderson
Managing Editor: Bridget Giles
Production Director: Alastair Gourlay
Editorial Director: Lindsey Lowe

Consultant Editor
Dr. Peter Mitchell is University Lecturer in African Prehistory, and holds a Tutorial Fellowship in Archaeology at St. Hugh's College, University of Oxford, United Kingdom. He is also Curator of African Archaeology at the Pitt Rivers Museum, Oxford, and an academic member of the multidisciplinary African Studies Centre based at St. Antony's College, Oxford. He has previously worked at the University of Cape Town. He serves on the Governing Council of the British Institute in Eastern Africa and is a member of the editorial boards of numerous journals. From 2004–2006 he held the post of President of the Society of Africanist Archaeologists.

Advisory Editor
Dr. David Johnson is University Lecturer in Comparative and International Education (Developing Countries) and a Fellow of St. Antony's College, University of Oxford, United Kingdom. He is a member of the African Studies Centre, based at St. Antony's College, and has conducted research into education in a wide range of African countries. He serves on the United Kingdom National Commission for UNESCO's working committee on Africa and on the editorial boards of two international journals.

Authors
Amy-Jane Beer
Matthew Davies
Anne Haour
Peter Mitchell
Darryl Wilkinson
Daniel Zimbler

Title page *A camel in front of the pyramids at Giza, Egypt.*

CONTENTS

NORTH AFRICA TODAY	4–5
PHYSICAL NORTH AFRICA	6–7
BIOMES OF NORTH AFRICA	8–9
PEOPLES OF NORTH AFRICA	10–11
CULTURES OF NORTH AFRICA	12–13
HISTORY	14–19
ARABIC LITERATURE	20–23
ARABS	24–29
ARCHITECTURE	30–33
BAGGARA	34–35
BEJA	36–37
BERBERS	38–41
CALLIGRAPHY	42–43
CHRISTIANITY	44–45
CONTEMPORARY ART	46–49
COPTS	50–51
DANCE AND SONG	52–55
DINKA	56–59
FESTIVAL AND CEREMONY	60–61
FRENCH-LANGUAGE LITERATURE	62–63
FUR	64–65
ISLAM	66–69
JEWS	70–71
LEATHERWORK	72–73
MARRIAGE AND THE FAMILY	74–75
METALWORK	76–77
MOVIES	78–79
MUSIC AND MUSICAL INSTRUMENTS	80–83
NUBA	84–87
NUBIANS	88–91
NUER	92–95
ORAL LITERATURE	96–98
SCULPTURE	99–101
SHILLUK	102–103
TELEVISION AND RADIO	104–105
TEXTILES	106–107
GLOSSARY	108–109
FURTHER RESOURCES	110
INDEX	111–112

Peoples and Cultures of Africa provides a region-based study of Africa's main ethnic groups, cultures, languages, religions, music, and much more. Five of the six volumes cover large geographical regions, namely: *North Africa, West Africa, East Africa, Central Africa*, and *Southern Africa*. Each of these volumes starts with a series of overview articles covering the political situation today, physical geography, biomes, peoples, cultures, and finally a historical time line. The main articles that follow are arranged A–Z with four types of articles, each distinguished by a characteristic running-head logo and color panel:

ETHNIC GROUPS, such as Maasai, Zulu, Yoruba. Each ethnic group article includes a Fact File and a map, giving the approximate area in which a people mainly live.

MATERIAL CULTURE, such as Contemporary Art, Metalwork, Sculpture, Textiles

PERFORMING ARTS AND LITERATURE, such as African-language Literature, Masks and Masquerade, Dance and Song

RELIGION, SOCIETY, AND CULTURE, such as Islam, Christianity, Marriage and the Family

The sixth volume (*Nations and Personalities*) is divided into three main sections: *Political and Physical Africa* presents a complete overview of Africa, followed by profiles of every nation on the continent; *International Organizations* and *Environmental Organizations* review major international bodies operating in the region; and *African Personalities* gives biographies of some 300 people from throughout Africa.

Within each volume there is a *Glossary* of key terms, lists of *Further Resources* such as other reference books, and useful Web sites. Volume *Indexes* are provided in volumes 1–5, with a complete *Set Index* in volume 6.

NORTH AFRICA TODAY

THERE IS A WIDE RANGE OF PEOPLES AND LIFESTYLES IN MODERN NORTH AFRICA. OFTEN GREAT VARIATION EXISTS WITHIN A RELATIVELY SMALL GEOGRAPHICAL AREA. ALONG THE NORTH COAST AND ON THE BANKS OF THE NILE ARE SOME OF THE MOST DENSELY POPULATED AND RAPIDLY GROWING URBAN CENTERS IN AFRICA, YET JUST BEYOND THESE BUSY CITIES LIE VAST EXPANSES OF DESERT, SPARSELY PEOPLED EXCEPT FOR SMALL GROUPS OF NOMADS.

Throughout the 20th century most of North Africa saw improvements in standards of living, health care, and sanitation. Average life expectancies are now relatively high compared with most African states, reaching 75 and 77 years of age in Tunisia and Libya respectively. Sudan is an exception to this general rule, experiencing a decline in living standards after decades of conflict, with a life expectancy of just 59 years. Access to health care and good living conditions are strongly linked to wealth and social status, and there are major disparities between rich and poor across the region.

Since the colonial period, rapid urban growth has been, and continues to be, a major feature of North Africa, along with significant overall population increases. In the 1960s around one-third of the population lived in towns, whereas today over a half of all people are city dwellers. Morocco, Tunisia, and Egypt have well-developed tourist industries that provide an income for large numbers of people and are major sources of foreign currency earnings. The economies of Algeria and Libya are heavily dependent on oil, especially the latter, whose oil revenues represent 80 percent of its gross domestic product.

One of the major tourist attractions in Egypt is the Great Pyramid at Giza. In recent decades, the country has promoted tourism as a major source of foreign income and of jobs.

A political map of North Africa. Many of the frontiers here show the influence of colonialism, with borders drawn straight across desert regions during the "Scramble for Africa" by European nations in the late 19th century.

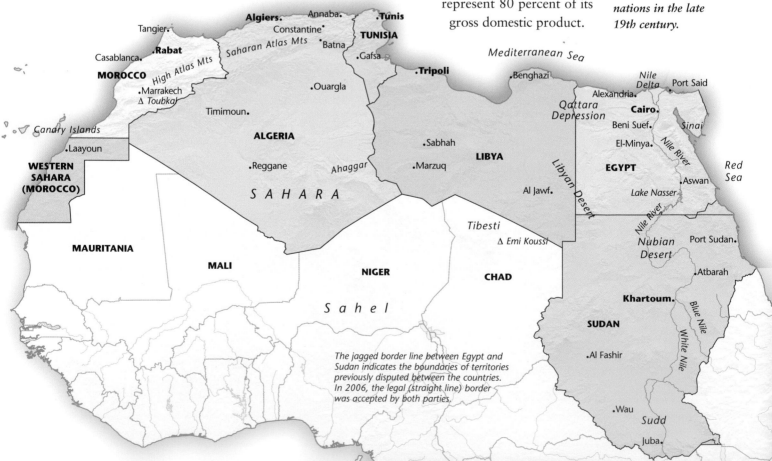

The jagged border line between Egypt and Sudan indicates the boundaries of territories previously disputed between the countries. In 2006, the legal (straight line) border was accepted by both parties.

POLITICAL DIFFICULTIES

Political instability has been an ongoing problem for several North African states in both the colonial and postindependence eras. Military coups have taken place in Algeria, Libya, and Sudan since independence. The republic established in Libya by Muammar Qaddafi in 1969 has had difficult relations with the international community. Allegations of support for international terrorism resulted in U.S. air strikes in 1987 and the imposition of UN trade sanctions in 1992. Since 2003, sanctions have been lifted and relations between Libya and the West have improved, alongside agreements to curb weapons programs and pay reparations to families who have suffered as a result of Libyan-sponsored terrorism. Islamist fundamentalists, who were responsible for the assassination of Egyptian President Anwar el-Sadat in 1981, have been involved in increasing violence in Egypt since the 1990s, including against tourists. This has prompted strict security measures by the government of Hosni Mubarak.

People fleeing the conflict in the Darfur region of Sudan in 2004 take shelter in a refugee camp in neighboring Chad.

SUDANESE CIVIL WARS

Sudan has suffered from violence and civil war since it achieved independence in 1956, except for a period of relative peace between 1972 and 1983. The most recent phase of the conflict, rooted in ethnic tensions between the Muslim, Arab-dominated north and the traditionally non-Muslim south, has cost 2 million lives and resulted in the displacement of some 4 million people.

In 2003 another crisis erupted, with attacks on non-Muslim populations in the western Sudanese province of Darfur by Arab militia groups known as the Janjaweed. This violence attracted international attention and condemnation. Peace talks in 2003–04 resulted in a cease-fire in southern Sudan and an agreement to grant autonomy and perhaps eventually independence to the southern provinces. However, violence still continues. It remains to be seen whether the coming years will bring about progress and establish lasting peace in what has been one of Africa's most troubled and violent regions.

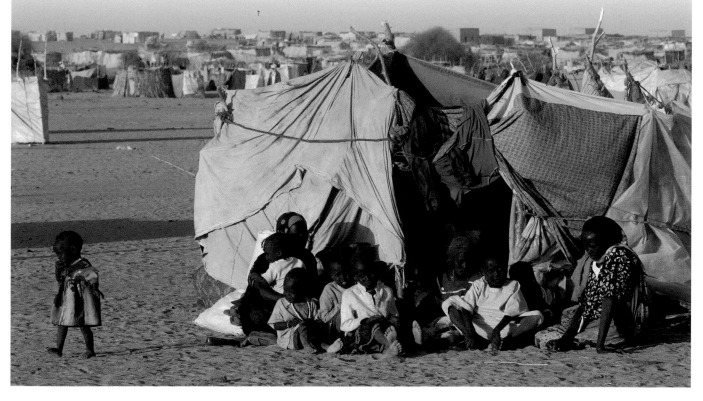

PHYSICAL NORTH AFRICA

NORTH AFRICA'S LANDSCAPE IS DOMINATED BY THE VAST AND STEADILY GROWING SAHARA. IN THE NORTHWEST THE DESERT GIVES WAY TO MOUNTAINS AND A WET COASTAL PLAIN. EAST OF THE SAHARA LIES THE NILE RIVER, WHOSE FERTILE DELTA WAS THE CRADLE OF THE ANCIENT EGYPTIAN CIVILIZATION.

THE SAHARA

Historically the Sahara has formed a barrier between coastal North Africa and sub-Saharan Africa. It is the largest desert on Earth, being almost equal in size to the entire United States. With a mean annual rainfall of 5 inches (127 mm), the Sahara is extremely arid, apart from occasional oases, and there are no permanent watercourses. However, some seasonally dry valleys (wadis) run with water during storms. The lack of rivers, which often form the borders between states elsewhere, has been significant in shaping the region's political geography. Unable to use rivers to mark the frontiers of the territories they had annexed, European colonists often drew straight lines on maps to define their possessions.

The immense seas of sand dunes, known as ergs, are the most powerful popular image of the desert. However, these make up only 15 percent of its total area. The rest is mostly bare rock and gravel, and the interior is much more mountainous. The highest point of the desert is Emi Koussi, at 11,204 ft (3,415 m) above sea level in the Tibesti Mountains in Chad. On the southern fringes of the Sahara, the desert gives way to the Sahel, a term that comes from the Arabic word for "shore." The Sahel is mainly semidesert scrubland, with higher levels of rainfall.

Map showing the main physical features of North Africa. The inhospitable Sahara is not impassable; major trans-Saharan trade flourished from around 1000 to 1800.

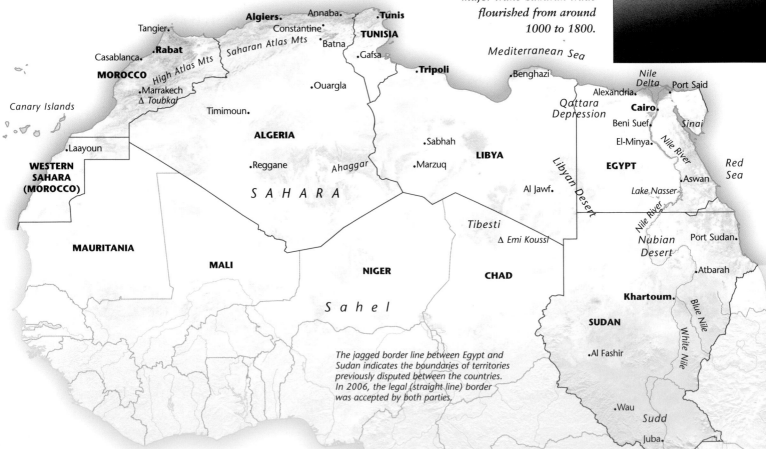

The jagged border line between Egypt and Sudan indicates the boundaries of territories previously disputed between the countries. In 2006, the legal (straight line) border was accepted by both parties.

One of the most significant physical features of the Nile River is artificial. Lake Nasser, a 300-mile- (483 km-) long reservoir, was formed in 1971 after completion of the Aswan High Dam. This major engineering project resulted in the resettlement of some 100,000 people living in the Nubian Valley, which was flooded by the impounded lake.

MOUNTAINS AND THE COAST

The most significant highland area in North Africa is the Atlas Mountains range, which runs for 1,200 miles (1,930 km) through Morocco, northern Algeria, and Tunisia, with the snowcapped peaks of the High Atlas range in Morocco reaching 13,000 feet (c.4,000 m) above sea level. To the south lies the Sahara and to the north, between the mountains and the sea, there is a fertile and well-watered plain where much agriculture takes place. This coastal plain has historically been the second most densely populated region of North Africa.

The remainder of the North African coast is generally more arid. However, pockets of coastal Tripolitania and Cyrenaica (in northern Libya) receive rainfall levels similar to parts of Mediterranean Europe.

THE NILE

The Nile River and its hinterland have historically been Africa's most populous and most agriculturally productive region. The lower (northern) reaches of the Nile form a narrow strip of fertile land running through the desert for some 750 miles (1,200 km) until the waters fan out into a delta on the Mediterranean coast. There, the shift from farmland on the banks of the river to the barren desert is marked. The area north of Aswan was historically known as Egypt, while the lands to the south as far as Khartoum were known as Nubia. The Nubian course of the Nile is less navigable than in Egypt and the landscape more varied, ranging from fertile floodplains to barren rock.

Sculpted by the winds, these crescent-shaped sand dunes in Fezzan, Libya, characterize the beautiful but forbidding landscape of the Sahara.

The Nile Delta seen from space. The great fertility of the soils washed down the Nile River allowed human settlement and culture to flourish here from early times.

BIOMES OF NORTH AFRICA

MUCH OF NORTH AFRICA IS SEPARATED FROM THE REST OF THE CONTINENT BY THE GREAT BARRIER FORMED BY THE SAHARA. THIS MAKES ITS CLIMATE AND ECOLOGY QUITE DIFFERENT. IN MANY PARTS OF THE REGION SEMIDESERT AREAS ARE INCREASING, MAKING ONCE-FERTILE LANDS BARREN. IN THE EAST, HUMAN ACTIVITY IS HAVING A PROFOUND IMPACT ON THE NILE VALLEY.

DESERT/XERIC SCRUB: THE SAHARA

The Sahara covers some 80 percent of North Africa. The landscape is a mix of sand dunes, flat gravel plains, rocky plateaus (*hammadas*), and seasonally dry valleys (wadis). Mean annual temperatures exceed 86°F (30°C), but there are dramatic seasonal and daily variations—from below freezing winter nights up to summer highs in excess of 122°F (50°C). Rain is infrequent and unreliable; in many areas none falls for years, then a sudden downpour may deliver 0.8 inches (20 mm) in a single day. Desert oases are places where groundwater rises from the rock, creating small, green pockets of life. Plant diversity is low (for example, date palms and carob trees), but animal life is surprisingly varied, with several species of large mammals, such as the critically endangered addax and the fennec (desert) fox, about 90 birds, including sand grouse and the hooded wheatear (unique to the region), and up to 100 reptiles, including the Saharan sand viper.

1

Animal species of North Africa: 1 Barbary macaque (Macaca sylvanus); 2 Striped Hyena (Hyaena hyaena); 3 Fennec fox (Vulpes zerda); 4 Nile crocodile (Crocodylus niloticus).

- Temperate coniferous forest
- Montane grassland
- Mediterranean scrub
- Deserts and xeric shrublands
- Tropical and subtropical grasslands, savannas, and shrubland
- Tropical and subtropical moist broadleaf forests
- Flooded grasslands
- Water

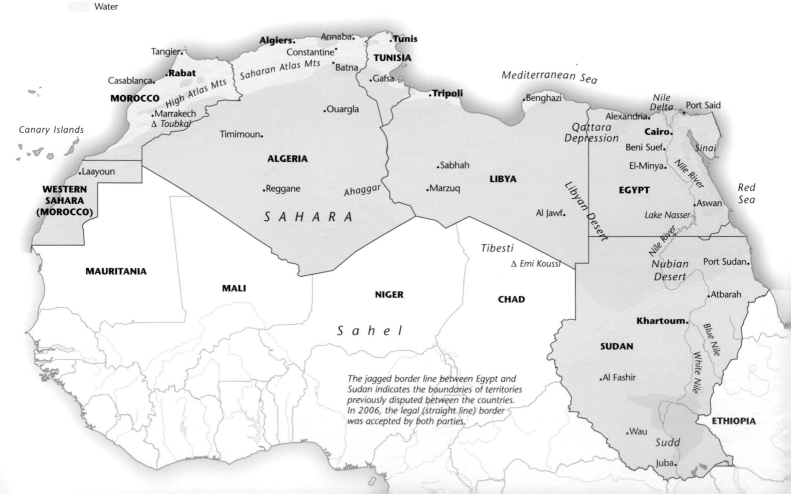

Tangier

Algiers · Annaba · · Tunis

Constantine · TUNISIA

Casablanca · · Rabat   Saharan Atlas Mts · Batna

MOROCCO   High Atlas Mts · Gafsa   · Tripoli   Mediterranean Sea   Benghazi   Nile Delta   Port Said

· Marrakech   · Ouargla   Alexandria ·   Qattara Depression   Cairo

Canary Islands   Δ Toubkal   Beni Suef ·   Sinai

Timimoun ·   ALGERIA   El-Minya ·   Nile River

· Laayoun   · Sabhah   LIBYA   EGYPT   Red Sea

WESTERN SAHARA (MOROCCO)   · Reggane   Ahaggar   · Marzuq   · Aswan   Lake Nasser

S A H A R A   Al Jawf ·   Libyan Desert

MAURITANIA   Tibesti   Δ Emi Koussi   Nubian Desert   Port Sudan ·

MALI   · Atbarah

NIGER   CHAD   Khartoum ·

S a h e l   SUDAN   Blue Nile   White Nile

The jagged border line between Egypt and Sudan indicates the boundaries of territories previously disputed between the countries. In 2006, the legal (straight line) border was accepted by both parties.

· Al Fashir

ETHIOPIA

· Wau   Sudd

Juba ·

drastically altered by hydroelectric schemes, notably the Aswan High Dam project. Floodwaters are now impounded in huge reservoirs. Yet the delta is still home to huge concentrations of gulls, terns, and waders and an important stopping point for millions of other birds during the spring and fall migration. Farther south, the White Nile is less restricted, and in southern Sudan regularly overflows into the largest floodplain in Africa. The area provides rich grazing for many large mammal and bird species, including shoebill storks.

TEMPERATE CONIFEROUS FOREST

Parts of northwest Africa have pockets of pine forest—dominated by Aleppo pine, cedar, and the ancient Berber thuya pine. South into the Atlas Mountains are ever dwindling stands of cypress. Characteristic birds and mammals of the region include golden eagles, caracal (a wildcat species), polecat ferrets, and Barbary macaques.

MONTANE GRASSLAND: HIGH ATLAS

The High Atlas Mountains are snow-covered for several months a year. Vegetation there includes sparse juniper woodland. The argan tree is valued for its olivelike fruit. Sheltered valleys in the mountains provide rich grazing pasture, and the region has long been farmed by Berber people.

MEDITERRANEAN SCRUB

Much of northern Morocco, Algeria, Tunisia, and Libya is classic Mediterranean scrub. The hot, rocky landscape sprouts a variety of herbs and shrubs adapted to dry conditions. Aleppo pine, juniper, and holly oak are widespread. There are also many plants unique to the region (endemic) including the Libyan cyclamen and Libyan strawberry tree. Animal life here includes red foxes, wild boar, and grass snakes.

TROPICAL GRASSLAND/SAVANNA

Most of the region's grassland is in Sudan, where years of civil war mean poaching is rife and conservation has a low priority. The landscape is hot and dry, dominated by tough grasses, including elephant grass. The area is home to many species of mammals, including the elephant, the African wild dog, and the cheetah, and two endemic birds, Reichenow's firefinch and Fox's weaver bird.

FLOODED GRASSLAND: THE NILE DELTA AND SUDD SWAMP

The Nile Delta was once a vast area of flooded grassland and papyrus swamp. In the 20th century the delta ecosystem was

Chebika oasis in the mountains of Tunisia. Oases only occur where there is an all-year-round supply of underground water. The date palm is the main source of food in oases.

PEOPLES OF NORTH AFRICA

THE MOST FAMOUS CIVILIZATION OF NORTH AFRICA IS THAT OF ANCIENT EGYPT, WHICH DEVELOPED FROM AROUND 4500 B.C.E. THE BERBERS SETTLED ON THE NORTH AFRICAN COAST IN C.3000 B.C.E., WHILE ON THE UPPER NILE THE NUBIAN KINGDOM OF KUSH HAD EMERGED BY C.2200 B.C.E.

In comparison with other regions of the continent, North Africa throughout its history has had relatively longer and more frequent contacts with Europe and Western Asia. With parts of it ruled by the Persians, Carthaginians, Greeks, or Romans, and later as all of it was greatly influenced by the spread of Islam, North Africa was very attractive to empire builders and traders. Moreover, Egypt has always had major interactions with the peoples of the eastern Mediterranean.

Throughout the Middle Ages, North Africa received major influxes of migrants from Muslim Arabia, and during the 19th and 20th centuries, significant numbers of Europeans also established settler colonies on the coast.

RELIGION

Islam is by far the most widely held faith of North Africa. Muslims in this region are followers of Sunni Islam, the majority branch of the religion, which recognizes the first four caliphs as the rightful successors of Muhammad. Adherence to Islam is nearly universal throughout the Maghreb (the northern coastal region) and among the peoples of the Sahara. Farther east, along the Nile and in the Sudan, the picture is more varied, although Islam is still the dominant religion in those areas. Sufism, a branch of Islam whose followers seek to gain a direct personal experience of God through devotion and prayer, is common among

Map showing the distribution of the population in North Africa. The highest concentrations of people are on the northwestern coastal strip, in the Nile Delta, and in southern Sudan, while the Sahara is very sparsely populated.

Population–people per 0.4 square miles (1 square km)

- 0–2
- 3–10
- 11–20
- 21–500
- 501–1000+

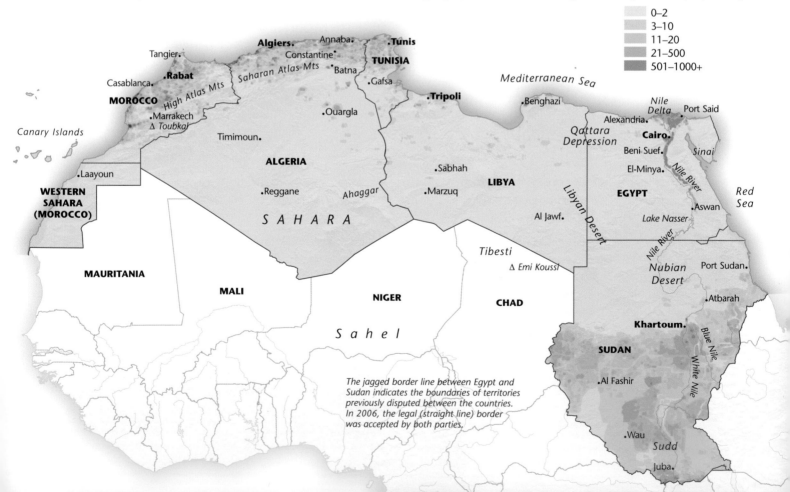

The jagged border line between Egypt and Sudan indicates the boundaries of territories previously disputed between the countries. In 2006, the legal (straight line) border was accepted by both parties.

livestock-herding peoples of North Africa, including Berbers and some Sudanese nomads.

The Coptic Church, an ancient branch of the Christian church, has a significant presence in Egypt, with approximately 10 million followers. Southern Sudan is inhabited by a variety of Nilotic peoples, such as the Nuer, Dinka, Nuba, and Shilluk, with a combined population of around 6 million, many of whom observe preexisting religious beliefs. However, a number of people in that region have converted to Christianity as a result of Roman Catholic and Protestant missions.

Before decolonization, North Africa was home to a significant population of Jews, numbering some 750,000 individuals. Since the 1950s, however, most have emigrated to Israel or Western Europe and now only 10,000 or so remain, principally in Morocco and Tunisia.

LANGUAGES

Afro-Asiatic Languages

Languages of this group are the most widely spoken in North Africa. They include Berber and Arabic. Some form of Arabic is spoken by a majority of people in all North African countries. Modern Standard Arabic is widely understood, especially among urban and educated populations. However, many dialects are used in day-to-day conversation.

Berber languages of the northern branch are spoken by around one-fifth of the population of the Maghreb, mostly in highland and rural parts of Morocco and Algeria. For example, Kabyle is spoken by some 7 million people in Algeria, while Tachelhit is the language of around 3 million inhabitants of central Morocco. Tamasheq, a separate form of Berber, is spoken by the nomadic Tuareg of the Sahara.

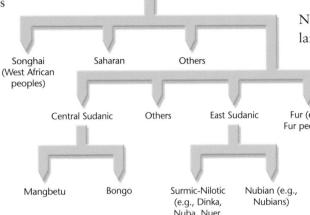

NILO-SAHARAN LANGUAGE FAMILY

Above and below: Summary family trees of the Nilo-Saharan and Afro-Asiatic language groups. The ethnic groups featured in this volume are listed in parentheses after the relevant language.

Some Muslim groups of eastern North Africa speak non-Arabic languages, such as To-Bedawiye, a Northern Cushitic language used by the Beja people.

Hebrew and Coptic, which are also Afro-Asiatic languages, are only spoken during the religious ceremonies of Jews and Coptic Christians respectively.

Nilo-Saharan Languages

These languages exhibit a great degree of diversity and are spoken by the indigenous peoples of southern Sudan and include the languages of groups such as the Nuer, Nuba, Shilluk, and the Dinka.

Other Languages

French is spoken by few people in North Africa as a mother tongue, except among North African Jews. However, due to the region's recent colonial past, French is quite widely understood in Algeria, Morocco, and Tunisia.

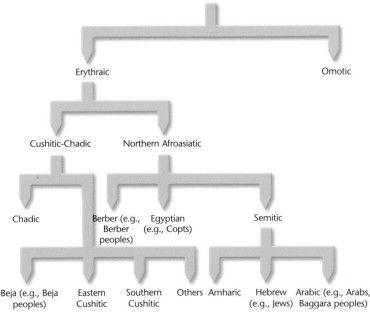

AFRO-ASIATIC LANGUAGE FAMILY

CULTURES OF NORTH AFRICA

THE CULTURES OF MODERN NORTH AFRICA REPRESENT A FUSION OF A WIDE RANGE OF INFLUENCES, AFFECTING ARTS, LITERATURE, SOCIETY, AND LANGUAGE. FROM THE SEVENTH CENTURY ON, THE CULTURE OF THE EASTERN ISLAMIC WORLD AND MUSLIM SPAIN CAME TO PLAY A MAJOR ROLE IN THE REGION, BECOMING ENTWINED WITH LOCAL TRADITIONS.

ARTS AND CRAFTS

North Africa is famous for its bustling marketplaces or souks, which sell an almost endless variety of items produced by local artisans, including textiles, ceramics, furniture, and jewelry. The area on the coast of northwest Africa known as the Maghreb is especially well known for its rugs and carpets, woven from wool produced by local sheep or dromedaries (camels) into regionally distinct patterns. Reflecting its Islamic and Berber origins, the crafts of North Africa are often highly ornate, decorated with elaborate repeating patterns and motifs that are painstakingly reproduced over and over again. These designs are notable for not depicting any living forms—an artistic practice banned by Islam. Instead, they focus on calligraphy, the creation of decorative scripts, often of verses from the Quran. Such items have been exported beyond North Africa for centuries and today are popular with tourists, who in many areas make up the largest market for craft goods.

Craft items produced by the Nilotic peoples of southern Sudan, such as the Nuer, Dinka, and Nuba, lack strong Islamic influences and therefore tend to be much less ornate, although no less skillful. The Nuer, for example, are noted for their fine

basketry, woodcrafts, and their manufacture of iron weaponry such as spears.

Modern North African artists widely use traditional crafts and art forms of the past as an inspiration for their work. For example, the Moroccan artist Farid Belkahia (b.1934) relies solely on local materials, using copper, wood, pottery, and lambskin in his art. He also uses many signs and characters from the Tifinagh, the alphabet used by the Tuareg and Berbers. The Tunisian artist Gouider Triki (b.1949) is famous for producing works that have been heavily influenced by the prehistoric rock art of the Sahara.

MUSIC AND DANCE

North African music is highly rhythmic and makes frequent use of improvization, incorporating folk elements, classical Islamic influences, and Western styles. Malouf, originally based on *qasidah*—the classical Arab poetry of Islamic Spain—and also incorporating Berber rhythms, is promoted as the national music of Tunisia by that country's government. Berber village music is commonly performed for dancing during ceremonial occasions such as weddings and is believed to offer protection from misfortune and evil spirits. It consists of chanted prayers and sung poetry set to music performed on flutes and drums.

Egypt has a well-established popular music industry, which has expanded significantly since the 1980s. Shaabi, originally derived from Egyptian folk music and influenced by Western pop, makes extensive use of synthesizers and electric guitars. It is produced for mainstream consumption and is popular in many other parts of North Africa as well.

LITERATURE

Thanks to the early arrival of Islam and its written culture in the region, North Africa has a far older tradition of literacy and written literature than any other part of the continent. As a result North Africa has produced much important modern writing in both Arabic and French. Arabic literature in North Africa is dominated by Egyptian writers such as Naguib Mahfouz (b.1911), who won the Nobel Prize for Literature in 1988, or Yusuf Idris (b.1927), famous for his short stories. Since the 1930s Tunisia has had a strong tradition of written poetry in Arabic.

The Maghreb, under the influence of pioneering writers such as Ahmed Sefrioui (b.1915), developed a vibrant body of French-language literature that became one of the major forums for expressing anticolonial views. In less urban regions of North Africa, oral rather than written literature continues to be extremely important. For example, there are strong storytelling and folklore traditions among the Berbers of the Maghreb and the peoples of southern Sudan.

The wool dyers' souk in Marrakech, Morocco. Trade across the Sahara from North to West Africa grew in scale from around 1000 C.E. onward, and many major cities grew up where important caravan routes crossed or ended.

GUANCHES

The Guanches were the precolonial inhabitants of Tenerife, the largest island in the Canary Islands, off the west coast of North Africa. Of North African origin and speaking a language related to that of the Berbers, they settled the Canaries in the 1st millennium B.C.E. and practiced farming there. They had some trading contacts with the Roman Empire and medieval Europe and North Africa before being colonized by Spain in the late 1300s and 1400s. In a pattern that was later repeated in the Caribbean and the Americas, many Guanches died after contact with European settlers, especially from epidemic disease or enslavement, while the remainder intermarried with Spanish settlers. Today, the culture of the Guanches is the inspiration for a small Canarian independence movement.

Caves formerly inhabited by the Guanches, the precolonial inhabitants of the Canary Islands. These people may have been related to the Berbers who still inhabit large parts of North Africa.

0.5 million years ago *Homo erectus* (an early form of human) is living in North Africa.

70,000 years ago Earliest evidence for modern humans in North Africa.

12,000 years ago The Sahara enters a wetter and more fertile phase. The rock paintings of the Tassili N'Ajer plateau are produced by hunter-gatherers.

9,500 years ago Herding of domestic animals begins to become established across North Africa.

7,500 years ago First farming communities established in the Nile valley.

c.3000 B.C.E. King Menes unifies Upper and Lower Egypt to found the 1st Dynasty.

c.2686–2125 B.C.E. The Old Kingdom in Egypt begins building pyramids.

c.2570 B.C.E. The Great Pyramid of Khufu and (a little later) the Sphinx are built at Giza.

2500–1500 B.C.E. The Nubian kingdom of Kerma emerges, challenging Egypt at times for control of the Nile Valley.

1550–1070 B.C.E. Egyptian New Kingdom sees Egypt at the height of its power and in control of Nubia as far as the Fourth Cataract of the Nile.

800 B.C.E. The Phoenicians from the eastern Mediterranean found several colonies on the North African coast, including Carthage and Utica in what is now Tunisia.

c.720 B.C.E. The Nubian kingdom under King Piankhy conquers Egypt and establishes the 25th Dynasty.

750 B.C.E. Greek colonies extend to North African coast (modern Libya).

656 B.C.E. Egypt is conquered by the Assyrian empire. Nubian power is forced to withdraw south of the First Cataract of the Nile.

525 B.C.E. Persian forces annex Egypt and Cyrenaica. Persian rulers reign as the 27th–31st Dynasties.

500s B.C.E. Carthage emerges as the center of a powerful maritime empire in the western Mediterranean.

332–325 B.C.E. Alexander the Great conquers Egypt and Cyrenaica. The city of Alexandria is founded on the Egyptian coast.

c.250 B.C.E. Berbers establish Mauretania and two Numidian kingdoms on the North African coast.

295 B.C.E. The Meroitic period begins in Nubia.

146 B.C.E. Carthage falls to Romans in the Third Punic War.

30 B.C.E. Egypt is annexed to the Roman empire.

200 C.E. Alexandria emerges as a major intellectual center of the early Christian Church.

313 The Edict of Milan establishes Christianity as one of the official religions of the Roman empire.

The pyramids at Giza, near the Egyptian capital Cairo, are the most well-known landmarks of the ancient Egyptian civilization, which flourished for almost 3,000 years.

320   The Meroitic period ends in Nubia.

450s   The Western Roman empire disintegrates and the western provinces of North Africa fall under the power of indigenous rulers. The Eastern Roman Empire endures and maintains its control over Egypt and Cyrenaica.

540   Christian kingdoms emerge in Nubia.

550–610 The Eastern Roman Empire reconquers much of North Africa as far as Algeria.

622   The prophet Muhammad founds Islam in what is now Saudi Arabia. On his death (632), his followers begin to found an Islamic empire, which by 641 includes Egypt. Islam then spreads rapidly across North Africa.

647   Cyrenaica and Tripolitania are incorporated into the Islamic world.

by 711 The Maghreb is fully incorporated into the Islamic world, despite some Berber resistence. Islam is introduced to the Sanhaja, a Berber tribe of the Sahara that has trading links with West Africa.

750s   The trans-Saharan trade is established and intensifies over the following centuries. Regular links are forged between the Muslim North African coast and the indigenous states of West Africa.

912   The emergent Fatimid caliphate gains control over Tunisia and coastal Algeria, centered on the newly founded capital of Mahdiya (Tunisia).

969   Egypt falls to the Fatimids. The city of Cairo is founded and eventually becomes their new capital. Their western territories, Tripolitania, Tunisia, and Algeria, are ruled by an allied Sanhaja dynasty, the Zirids. The Zirids succeed in incorporating Morocco into their domain.

c. 975   Two groups of Bedouin nomads, the Sulaym and the Hilali, migrate from the Arabian peninsula into the Egyptian Eastern Desert.

980   Morocco breaks away from Zirid-Fatimid control.

1049   The Zirid principalities of Algeria and Tunisia–Tripolitania break their alliance with the Fatimids.

1050s   Bedouins, encouraged by the Fatimids, migrate along the North African coast, conquering the Zirids, except for a few pockets of resistance. In the west, the Sanhaja Berbers, inspired by the puritanical Almoravid sect, seize control of the western Saharan trade routes and Morocco. By the end of the century they also control southern Spain.

The famous Arab leader Saladin (or Salah ud-Din; 1137–93) conquered Egypt in 1171 for the Syrian Zangid dynasty, and became its Sultan. He used Egypt's agricultural wealth to finance a campaign that spread his rule across the Middle East. Saladin founded the Ayyubid dynasty, which ruled Egypt for 80 years.

1150s   The Almoravid empire collapses, with the Sanhaja replaced in Morocco by the Zenata Berbers as the dominant power. The Zenata establish the Almohad empire over the Maghreb and southern Spain.

1171   Saladin overthrows the Fatimids in Egypt and establishes the Ayyubid dynasty.

1230s   The Almohad empire contracts and breaks up into three smaller fiefdoms.

1250   The Mamlukes, originally the Turkish slaves making up the Ayyubid armies, take control of Egypt.

c. 1320 Juhayna Bedouin migrate into Nubia, settling along the Nile between the Second and Sixth Cataracts. Others settle farther west in Kordofan and Darfur.

1325–53 Ibn Battuta, the celebrated Moroccan traveler and writer, undertakes his travels throughout the Islamic world, including North and West Africa.

The first intervention of a modern Western power in North Africa came in 1798, when the French commander Napoleon Bonaparte invaded Egypt to threaten Britain's trade routes to India. The French seized Alexandria (above) and routed a Mamluke army at the Battle of the Pyramids but were soon defeated by the British.

1415 The Portuguese seize Ceuta on the Mediterranean coast of Morocco.

1471 The Portuguese make use of the opportunity provided by the Marinid–Wattasid civil war in Morocco to capture further territory in North Africa.

1504 The Funj kingdom is founded in what is now southern Sudan.

1517 The Ottoman Turks overthrow the Mamlukes in Egypt and capture Cyrenaica. Tensions arise between the Ottomans and the Spanish over control of the North African coast in the western Mediterranean.

1550 Most people in Nubia have converted to Islam, and the region passes from Christian to Muslim rule.

1574 The Ottomans establish their authority over the areas of Tripolitania, Tunisia, and Algeria that had been contested by Spain.

1578 The Portuguese suffer a major defeat at the hands of Moroccan forces at Alcazar el Kebir, and are forced to withdraw from most of their territory in Morroco.

1591 Morocco, under the leadership of Almansur ("the victorious") conquers the West African Songhai empire, forming an empire that stretches from the coast to the bend of the Niger River.

c.1600 The Arab sultanate of Darfur is established in the territory of the Fur people.

c.1660 The trans-Saharan empire of Morocco disintegrates.

1705–14 Algiers, Tunis, and Tripolitania achieve independence from the Ottoman empire.

1798 Egypt falls to Napoleonic France, but British forces successfully force the French to withdraw within two years.

1811   Tripoli occupies the Fezzan oases in the Sahara in an effort to control the Tripoli–Bornu trade route.

1811–20 Mehmet Ali, a Turkish general, takes control of Egypt. He modernizes the army, eliminating its traditional feudal structure. Under Ali, Egypt undergoes imperialist expansion, incorporating Nubia and organizing slave raids against the Dinka and Nuer peoples of Sudan.

1830   Algiers falls to French forces.

1840   The French expand their North African possessions to include much of coastal Algeria.

1842   The Ottomans retake Tripoli's territories, including the Fezzan oases.

1847   The French finally defeat local resistance to the occupation of Algeria.

1875   Ismail, ruler of Egypt, sells his interests in the Suez canal to the British to lessen the financial crisis caused by his military over-expansion. This succeeds only in the short term, and Egypt becomes an international protectorate of its European creditors.

Under Mehmet Ali (1769–1849), who became viceroy of Egypt in 1811, Egypt moved away from Ottoman (Turkish) control, and became a strong regional power. His armies conquered the Sudan, where he founded the capital Khartoum in 1823.

In the late 1870s, Arab nationalists led by Urabi Pasha (1839–1911) began to agitate against European intervention in Egypt. As rioting spread, Britain sent an expeditionary force that defeated the nationalists at the Battle of Tel el-Kebir (above) in 1882. That same year, Egypt became a British protectorate.

1881   A nationalist uprising occurs in Egypt in a reaction to European control. British forces defeat the uprising by the following year. Mahdist forces in Sudan conquer previously Egyptian territory as far as the Second Cataract.

1885–1900 In the European colonial "Scramble for Africa," Algeria and Tunisia fall under French control. Britain takes Egypt and much of the Red Sea coast.

1895   French forces establish themselves in the area around Lake Chad, thereby linking up French North Africa (Algeria and Tunisia) with the French territories of West and Central Africa.

1898   British forces defeat the Mahdist state. Egypt, Sudan, (except Darfur) and much of the eastern Sahara fall under the British sphere of influence during the Scramble for Africa. The Anglo-Egyptian Condominium (joint administration) of the Sudan is founded in 1899.

1911   France and Spain divide up Morocco, the vast majority going to France.

1912   Coastal Tripolitania and Cyrenaica fall to Italian forces, although most of the North African interior remains independent.

1916   The sultanate of Darfur, which had fought against the allies in World War I, is annexed by British forces.

1928   Italy defeats the Bedouin insurgents of the Libyan interior. The Muslim Brotherhood, the first Islamic fundamentalist organization, is founded in Egypt to promote Islamic culture and oppose British imperialism.

1943   Britain defeats Italian forces and the German Afrika Korps in the North African campaign of World War II (1939–45). The former Italian territory of Libya is divided between Britain and France.

1945   The Arab League, an organization of Arab states, is founded.

1947   Decolonization begins. The British withdraw from Egypt except for the Suez Canal.

1951   Libya—consisting of Tripolitania, Cyrenaica, and the Fezzan area of the Sahara—gains independence from the British under King Idris al-Sanusi.

1952   King Farouk of Egypt is overthrown in a military coup and flees the country.

1954   In Algeria, war breaks out between French forces, acting on behalf of more than 1 million European settlers, and the Algerian Liberation Front representing the majority of the Muslim population.

1956   The Suez canal is nationalized by Egypt under President Gamal Abdel Nasser. The British and French intervene in an effort to prevent this, but are forced to withdraw under UN pressure. Morocco, Sudan, and Tunisia gain independence. Tensions between the Muslim north and the non-Muslim south in Sudan develop into a state of civil war.

1958   General Abboud takes power in Sudan after a military coup.

1962   France finally abandons its attempts to retain Algeria. President Ahmed Ben Bella takes power. The Anyana movement is formed in southern Sudan to fight against the government, resulting in an intensification of the conflict.

1963   The building of the Aswan High Dam on the Nile, which creates the huge Lake Nasser, displaces many Nubians and ends the annual flooding of the Nile. The Organization of African Unity (OAU) is founded.

1965   A military coup under Colonel Houari Boumedienne in Algeria establishes a one-party socialist state.

1969   Colonel Muammar Qaddafi rises to power in Libya and overthrows the monarchy there. The Libyan oil industry is nationalized and production is expanded.

French troops going ashore at Port Fuad, Egypt, during the Suez Crisis of 1956. This ill-fated Western intervention increased support for Egyptian President Nasser's Arab nationalism.

1970   Egyptian leader Gamal Abdel Nasser dies and is succeeded by Anwar Sadat.

1973   The first phase of the Sudanese Civil War ends; the Yom Kippur War erupts, as Egypt and Syria attack Israel to avenge defeat in the Six-Day War of 1967.

1975   Western Sahara region is ceded to Morocco and Mauritania by its former colonial ruler Spain.

1981   Nasser's successor, President Anwar Sadat of Egypt, is assassinated by Islamist extremists; he is succeeded by Hosni Mubarak.

1983   The Sudanese civil war resumes as the Sudanese government imposes Sharia (Islamic law) against the wishes of the people of the south.

1986   The U.S. conducts air raids on Libya in response to allegations of support for terrorist organizations.

1988   Multiparty politics are instituted in Tunisia. Economic crisis brings increasing unrest in Algeria.

1989   An Islamist military regime is established in Sudan, resulting in increased levels of violence against the non-Muslim populations in the southern Sudan.

1990s Sporadic terrorist attacks on Copts and their churches, especially in middle Egypt, are carried out by extreme Islamists.

1990   Famine in Sudan threatens the lives of 8 million people; Berbers demonstrate in Algeria after the Berber language is outlawed.

1991   Fearing victory by popular radical Islamist parties, the Algerian government cancels elections, sparking several years of serious unrest; cease-fire in Western Sahara between Polisario Front guerrillas fighting since 1975 for independence and Moroccan forces.

1992   U.N. imposes sanctions on Libya due to its suspected involvement in bombing a U.S. airliner in 1988.

1994   Libya and Chad sign a peace agreement that ends a 20-year border dispute.

1995   Egyptian President Hosni Mubarak survives assassination attempts and cracks down on Islamist extremists.

1997   Gunmen of the radical Gamaa al-Islamiya group kill 65 tourists at the Temple of Hatshepshut at Luxor, Egypt.

1999   Multiparty politics revived in Sudan but suspended the same year, and a state of emergency is declared.

Refugees in southern Sudan in 1993. Since independence in 1956, Sudan has been plagued by civil war and genocide, arising from tensions between the Arab, Islamic north—the seat of the government—and the mainly Christian south.

2003   Violence erupts in Darfur, a province in western Sudan. United Nations sanctions against Libya are lifted following from an agreement to curb nuclear and chemical weapons programs and pay damages to victims of Libyan-sponsored terrorism; in Morocco, a group linked to al-Qaeda bombs Western and Jewish targets in Casablanca, killing 33 people.

2004   After a period of negotiations a cease-fire is implemented in Sudan, although this is not accepted by all groups and violence continues in Darfur.

2005   Sudanese People's Liberation Army leader John Garang, a Dinka, signs a peace accord with the Khartoum government, and is appointed vice-president but dies in a helicopter crash.

MAJOR WORKS AND THEIR AUTHORS

Title	Date	Author	Country
Zaynab	1913	Muhammad Husayn Haykal	Egypt
Egyptian Childhood	1932	Taha Hussein	Egypt
Ahl al-Kahf	1933	Tawfiq al-Hakim	Egypt
The People of the High Dam	1967	Raouf Musad	Sudan
Kuss Ummiyat	1969	Naguib Surur	Egypt
Woman at Point Zero	1977	Nawal el-Saadawi	Egypt
Akhenaten, Dweller in Truth	1985	Naguib Mahfouz	Egypt
Doing Daily Battle	1991	Fatema Mernissi	Morocco
Memory in the Flesh	1998	Ahlam Mosteghanemi	Algeria
Roses and Ashes	2000	Mohammed Choukri	Morocco

LITERATURE IN THE ARABIC LANGUAGE HAS A LONG AND PROUD HISTORY STRETCHING BACK SEVERAL CENTURIES. MANY NORTH AFRICAN WRITERS AFTER INDEPENDENCE WROTE IN FRENCH, BUT MODERN ARABIC LITERATURE IS INCREASINGLY GAINING GROUND.

HISTORY

The earliest known Arabic literature was produced in northern Arabia in around 500 C.E. and took the form of oral poetry, memorized and recited aloud. These traditions spread across North Africa with the Arab conquests during the seventh and eighth centuries, where they began to be set down in writing. Arabic prose, as a literary

Copies of the Quran and other Islamic works on sale in Morocco. The urge to make the sacred text of Islam available to as many people as possible was the main driving force behind the creation and widespread adoption of written forms of Arabic.

This beautifully illustrated manuscript (left) of a medieval Arabic poem, the Romance of Varqa and Guishah, *comes from 13th-century Turkey. The spread of Arabic culture across the Middle East, including North Africa, meant that there was a lively interchange of culture throughout the Islamic world from an early date.*

form, was developed during the late eighth and early ninth centuries. Its originators are believed to have been the class of Persian officials who served as scribes to the Abbasid caliphs (750–1256) in their capital Baghdad.

As part of the culture of the wider Arabic world, both poetry and prose flourished across North Africa throughout the Middle Ages. Also popular were factual and historical accounts. For example, during the 14th century, the North African traveler Ibn Battuta (1304–69) wrote famous accounts of his travels to places as far-flung as sub-Saharan West and East Africa. The historical and philosophical works of the North African historian Ibn Khaldun (1332–1406) are also of great significance.

Following the French invasion of Egypt under Napoleon Bonaparte in 1798, new European literary styles found their way into North Africa. Today modern North African literature presents an interesting mix of styles and traditions, including biographies, short stories, and novels. The first Arabic novel is generally considered to be *Zaynab* (1913) by the Egyptian writer Muhammad Husayn Haykal, which tells the story of a peasant girl who is a victim of social conventions. Also, the early autobiography of Taha Hussein, *al-Ayyam* (The Days), is widely regarded as a masterpiece of modern Arabic prose.

ARABIC POETRY

Arabic poetry has a long history and it remains one of the most highly respected art forms in the Arabic speaking world. The meters—that is, the rhythm and the number of beats—used in Arabic poetry were recorded during the eighth century by al-Khalil bin Ahmad and have changed little since. The meter (*wazn*) is based on the length of the syllable and distinguishes between long and short syllables. Each line is divided into two halves, which should be read from left to right. Arabic poetry often incorporates rhyme which is determined by the last consonant of the word. Originally older poetry, such as the *qasidah* (ode), made use of a single rhyme that may have been carried for more than a hundred lines or more. Later, more varied rhyme schemes were developed and today highly complex patterns can be employed.

MODERN ARABIC WRITERS

Although state censorship and low levels of literacy have restricted literary activity in many Arab countries, North Africa has still produced a steady stream of respected novelists, biographers, and playwrights, whose works deserve greater exposure in the West. Egypt, in particular, can boast a wealth of literary talent. Other North African countries that were once under French colonial rule have also made significant contributions—despite the fact that many of their authors choose to write in French rather than Arabic in order to reach a larger audience.

Naguib Mahfouz, the "grand old man" of Arabic letters, is a socially committed writer whose works expose injustices. His 32 novels and 13 collections of short stories have found a broad popular readership, both at home in Egypt and abroad.

EGYPT

Perhaps the most celebrated and exceptional Arabic writer of the 20th century, the Egyptian Naguib Mahfouz (b.1911) won the Nobel Prize for Literature in 1988 (see box feature). He has written a wide variety of literary works spanning six decades, including novels, plays, and screenplays, from *Whispers of Madness* (1938) to *Akhenaten, Dweller in Truth* (1985).

Naguib's compatriot Taha Hussein (1889–1973) was a literary scholar and figurehead of the modernist movement in Egypt. Hussein was the first graduate to receive a doctoral degree from the nonreligious Cairo University, founded in 1908. Despite being blind from an early age, he wrote several novels and essays. However, he is best known for his three-volume autobiography, which has been published in English as *Egyptian Childhood* (1932), *The Stream of Days* (1943), and *A Passage to France* (1976).

Tawfiq al-Hakim (1898–1987) was born in Alexandria as the son of a wealthy judge, and studied in Cairo and Paris before taking up law and journalism. Although he wrote novels and poems he is best known for his prolific plays which range from *Ahl Al-Kahf* (1933; People of the Cave), to *Al-Hamir* (1975, The Donkeys). Translated works of his include *Fate of a Cockroach and Other Plays* (1980).

The writer Naguib Surur (1932–78) was a controversial character who intended his works to shock as much as to entertain. Surur was a poet, playwright, actor, director, and critic. His most famous work is the poem *Kuss Ummiyyat* (1969). This darkly satirical attack on official culture combines a stream of abuse with wonderful lyricism. It remains banned in Egypt.

The Egyptian feminist writer and activist Nawal el-Saadawi (b.1931) has written widely on the plight of women in Arab society. In 1981 she was imprisoned by the Egyptian authorities for her vocal opposition to the Camp David peace accords with Israel, signed two years earlier, but was later released. In 2005 el-Saadawi considered running for the Egyptian presidency before pulling out in the face of strong criticism. Her most widely known book is *Woman*

NAGUIB MAHFOUZ

Naguib Mahfouz is probably the best known Arabic novelist of the 20th century. He is most famous for his critically acclaimed series of works *al-Thulathiyya* (The Cairo Trilogy), comprising the novels *Bayna al-Qasrayn* (1956; Palace Walk), *Qasr al-Shawq* (1956; Palace of Desire), and *al-Sukkariyah* (1957; Sugar Street). It chronicles the life of an Egyptian family. Another of Mahfouz's well-known works, *Children of Gebelawi* (1959), is banned in Egypt; in 1994, there was even an assassination attempt on the author's life by a religious extremist. Throughout his career Mahfouz has published more than 30 novels and in 1988 he was awarded the Nobel Prize for Literature.

at Point Zero (1977), which has been translated into English and several other languages.

Originally trained as a dentist, Alaa al-Aswani (b.1957) has written regularly for Egyptian newspapers on literature, social issues, and politics. His 2002 novel *Imarat Yaacoubian* (The Yacoubian Building) was the best-selling novel in Arabic for many years. It relates the problems of modern Egypt through the stories of the residents of a crumbling Cairo apartment block.

Yusuf Idris (1927–91) is regarded as a master of the Arabic short story. Idris writes powerfully on the themes of sexuality and male and female roles. One of his best known translated works is *City of Love and Ashes* (2002).

MOROCCO

A well-known Moroccan writer is the feminist Fatema Mernissi (b.1940). Born in Fez, Mernissi has written widely on the representation of women in the Quran and has written outspoken criticisms of the oppression of women. Her first book, *The Veil and the Male Elite: A Feminist Interpretation of Islam* (1988) is a powerful historical study of the role of the wives of Muhammad. Her other works include *Doing Daily Battle: Interviews with Moroccan Women* (1991) and her autobiography *Dreams of Trespass: Tales of Harem Girlhood* (1994).

Mohammed Choukri (1935–2003) was a Moroccan novelist and author of short stories. Completely self-taught, Choukri's early life was blighted by vagrancy, petty crime, and drug abuse; he exposed this underworld in his first, autobiographical book *For Bread Alone* (1972), which caused a sensation in the Arab world for its frankness. His later works included *Streetwise* (1992), *The Tent* (a collection of short stories, 1985), *Roses and Ashes* (2000), and *Wujuh* (2000).

ALGERIA

Ahlam Mosteghanemi, the daughter of Algerian revolutionary leader Mohammed Chérif, was the first female Algerian writer to have her works translated into English. To date, the first two of a trilogy have been translated. They are *Memory in the Flesh* and *Chaos of the Senses*. The trilogy deals with postcolonial Algeria's struggles for stability and development.

SUDAN

Raouf Musad (b.1937) was born in Port Sudan to Egyptian parents. He has traveled and lived in various Arab and European countries. In the 1950s and 1960s he was imprisoned in Egypt for communist agitation, and then spent many years abroad. In 1990 he moved permanently to the Netherlands. Musad established a small publishing house in 2004, dedicated to releasing the works of Arab writers. His first novel was *The People of the High Dam* (1967), while his novel *Ostrich Egg* (1994) has been translated into Spanish, French, English, and Italian.

SEE ALSO: Arabs; Contemporary art; French-language literature; Movies; Oral literature.

As well as writing about the position of women in Egyptian society, the author Nawal el-Saadawi is a trained doctor who has done humanitarian work in rural communitiues to improve women's lives. Her challenging ideas have brought her imprisonment by the authorities and death threats from extremists.

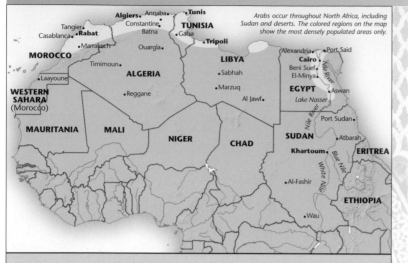

Arabs occur throughout North Africa, including Sudan and deserts. The colored regions on the map show the most densely populated areas only.

FACT FILE

Population	Egypt 64,000,000; Algeria 27,000,000; Sudan 22,000,000; Morocco 18,800,000; Tunisia 10,000,000; Libya 4,200,000
Religion	Sunni Islam
Language	Arabic, an Afro-Asiatic language, is spoken by most Arabs; there are several dialects. Modern Standard Arabic is used in the media and education.

TIMELINE

640–711 Arab armies conquer Egypt and steadily expand across North African coast to Morocco.

912–69 The Fatimid dynasty gains control of Tunisia, Algeria, and Egypt. Cairo is established as the Fatimid capital.

975–1050s Sulaym and Hilali Bedouin spread across North Africa.

1260 The Turkish Mamlukes rise to power in Egypt; Arab rule ends over much of North Africa.

1320s Juhayna Bedouin settle in Nubia and northern Sudan.

1517–74 The Ottoman Empire overruns much of North Africa.

1705–14 Western North Africa secedes from Ottoman Empire.

1840 The French establish their colony of Algeria.

1882–83 Egypt falls under British control; France annexes Tunisia.

1950s Many North African countries gain independence, reestablishing Arab rule for the first time in centuries.

1962 French withdraw from Algeria. Civil war intensifies in Sudan between Arab north and African south (to 1973).

1967 Arab coalition defeated by Israel in the Six-Day War.

1983 The Sudanese civil war resumes (to 2005).

2003 The Darfur conflict erupts in western Sudan.

THE ARABS ONCE LIVED SOLELY ON THE ARABIAN PENINSULA. FROM THE SEVENTH CENTURY ONWARD THEY SPREAD FAR BEYOND THEIR ORIGINAL HEARTLAND DURING THE ISLAMIC CONQUESTS, SETTLING WIDELY ACROSS NORTH AFRICA AND OTHER PARTS OF THE MIDDLE EAST. TODAY THEY ARE THE DOMINANT ETHNIC AND CULTURAL GROUP IN NORTH AFRICA.

HISTORY

It was on the Arabian Peninsula, in the cities of Mecca and Medina, that Islam originated and the Prophet Muhammad, the founder of Islam, taught the message of the Muslim holy book, the Quran. Although Muhammad died in 632 C.E., he had succeeded in converting many Arabs to Islam, and from the 630s onward, his followers carried this religion into North Africa through an impressive series of military victories. Egypt was the first to fall to the Islamic armies, in 640–42, and by 711 all of North Africa as far west as Morocco were brought under the control of the Islamic Empire. Although the Arabs who led the conquests were quickly able to bring the different areas of North Africa under their control, they would initially have made up only a small minority of the North African population. Most people in the region at that time were Christians and Berbers. Over the following centuries, there was a long process of Arabization in North Africa in which the various conquered peoples adopted the language and religion of their rulers.

During the Middle Ages, several major migrations of Muslim Arab nomads from the Arabian Peninsula into North Africa took place. In the 10th and 11th centuries,

Bedouin Arabs ride camels across the arid Sinai desert, Egypt. The nomadic, herding lifestyle of the Bedouin is increasingly under threat from dwindling grazing lands and government pressure encouraging or forcing them to settle.

the Benu Sulaym and Benu Hilali entered Egypt and spread along the North African coast, settling in Tunisia and Tripolitania (modern Algeria) in large numbers. These camel-herding Arabs, who were known as Bedouin, were easily able to adapt to life in the Sahara, accustomed as they were to living in the deserts of Arabia. They were the ancestors of the present-day Bedouin of North Africa. Later in the 14th century, the nomadic Juhayna Arabs who had settled in Egypt undertook a major expansion southward, pushing into Nubia and the

THE MOORS

The term *Moor* has had a variety of meanings throughout history. The word is originally Greek, and comes from the name of the Roman Province of Mauretania, which was located along the coast of Morocco and Algeria (not to be confused with the modern country Mauritania). In 711 the Arab and Berber armies of the Maghreb (western North Africa) conquered most of Spain and Portugal, forming the Islamic territory of al-Andalus (Andalusia). Spain was not fully reconquered by the Christian armies of Europe until 1492. The Christians of Europe called the Muslims who ruled Spain *Moors*. The most famous Moor in literature is Othello, a character in the English writer William Shakespeare's play of the same name (1604), who is described as being black. The Muslim inhabitants of Spain and the Maghreb were actually of mixed Berber and Arab heritage. However, most Europeans at the time *Othello* was written were not familiar enough with other ethnic groups to recognize any significant difference between an African, a Moor, or any other Muslim. Today the name *Moor* is applied to the mixed Arab–Berber peoples of Mauritania in northwest Africa who speak the Hassaniya dialect of Arabic, and who number some 3 million people.

rest of southern Sudan and mixing with local peoples. These were the ancestors of a number of Arab nomadic peoples such as the Baggara who live in that region today. In the initial conquests of the seventh century, the Arab influence had been largely confined to the urban centers and the coast. However, the later Arab migrations were largely responsible for bringing Islam and Arab culture to the desert and countryside.

The period from the 15th century on witnessed increasing European involvement in North Africa. The Spanish conquered parts of Morocco as early as the 1400s, while the French invaded Egypt in 1798. From the 1830s the French colonized Algeria, settling there in large numbers. By the early 20th century, North Africa had mostly been carved up by a number of colonial powers. France, and to a lesser extent Spain, controlled the Maghreb, and Egypt and Sudan were under British rule.

The effects of colonialism on the Arab populations of North Africa were profound. Especially in French-dominated regions such as Algeria, the Europeans introduced many cultural influences, such as their language and architecture. Yet the early 20th century also brought increasing resistance to European rule and a growing popular belief in the cause of Arab nationalism. The nations of North Africa finally achieved their independence during the 1950s and 1960s. The postcolonial period has seen attempts to promote solidarity between Arab states, especially in Egypt. Since the 1970s, Islamism has become increasingly prominent in North Africa. This political-religious movement is devoted to restoring conservative Islamic values and Islamic law, and ending Western influence in the Muslim

A bustling market in Algeria. People of different ethnicities have mixed for centuries in North Africa. Many Arabs feel that their identity is expressed through a shared culture comprising a common language, literature, religion, and history.

world. An Islamist government has come to power in Sudan, while violent Islamist movements oppose the secular (nonreligious) governments of Egypt and Algeria (see ISLAM).

SOCIETY AND DAILY LIFE

Arabs make up the vast majority of the North African population. With such a large group of people, it is unsurprising that there is a great variation in how they lead their day-to-day lives. Most Arabs fall into three broad categories: the urban populations that inhabit the major towns and cities of North Africa, the rural villagers who farm in the more fertile and irrigated regions, and the desert-dwelling nomadic Bedouin. Differences in social standing are strongly pronounced in Arab societies in North Africa, with the wealthiest families being concentrated in the major cities and particularly in the capitals. Urban elites are generally more educated and are involved in a wide range of occupations, including, politics, industry, teaching, the media, and tourism. Although most of the people living in cities cannot be counted among the wealthy, they still enjoy far higher standards of living, hygiene, and health care than those who live in the countryside. The urban working class tend to live in the older and more run-down quarters and often have more poorly paid jobs in tourism and industry, or find work as manual laborers and cleaners.

A majority of Arabs across North Africa are still involved in farming, although since the 20th century, the numbers of people who have migrated to the cities in search of work has increased massively. There are now almost as many people living in towns as in the countryside. Those who inhabit well-irrigated regions, such as the Nile Valley or the Moroccan coastal plain, generally enjoy greater prosperity and more reliable access to water than those who farm in drier areas.

THE WESTERN SAHARA

The Western Sahara is a disputed region in western North Africa. It borders on the Atlantic and lies between Morocco to the north and Mauritania to the south. Its population of 273,000 are mostly Arabs and Berbers. In the late 19th century the territory was a Spanish coastal enclave known as Rio de Oro, which was extended inland in the 20th century to create the colony of Spanish Sahara. The Spanish finally withdrew in 1975, and over the following three years the region was annexed by Morocco. Since then Morocco's control over the region has been challenged by the Polisario Front guerrilla movement. Polisario's aim is to gain independence for the Western Sahara, and in 1967 it formed a government in exile under the leadership of Mohamed Abdelaziz. In 1991 a cease fire was agreed, but this has not led to any permanent settlement between Morocco and the Polisario Front. However, 55 countries, including Algeria and Libya, already recognize the Western Sahara as an independent state.

Important crops include barley, wheat, olives, and fruits and vegetables. Sheep, goats, and cattle are also kept as livestock. Farmers on well-irrigated land tend to favor fruits and vegetables, keep fewer animals, and are able to supplement their income by harvesting and selling cash crops, such as cotton and beet sugar. Poorer farming families are often unable to grow enough food from their land, and outside of the agricultural season many are forced to migrate to the towns and cities to find temporary work as laborers. Many villagers have abandoned rural ways of life in order to find a more secure economic future in the cities. This process has contributed to the rapid growth of cities in North Africa over the course of the 20th and 21st centuries.

The Bedouin make up an increasingly small section of the Arab population and are generally confined to the more arid regions. There, agriculture is either not possible or is

An Arab boy drives his donkey cart past a tank abandoned by the Polisario Front during fighting against Moroccan forces over control of the disputed Western Sahara region.

not sufficient to meet daily needs. The Bedouin are nomads, whose livestock are their main source of food. This means that they have to move frequently to seek fresh grazing land. As a result the Bedouins' life is highly mobile and possessions are limited to what can be easily carried, including a tent and cooking utensils. There is considerable variation in how the Bedouin of North Africa lead their lives. Some, like those living in the drier Saharan interior, are much more nomadic and keep camels as their principal livestock. Others, such as the Bedouin who live in Sudan, Egypt's Western Desert, and Cyrenaica (northern Libya) keep cattle, which require richer pastures. These groups are also more likely to grow some crops.

The Bedouin have long resisted any state interference in their affairs. Although influential men called sheikhs exist in Bedouin society, they seldom recognize any authority beyond their own family group. However, the Bedouin have been subjected to greater state influence since the mid-20th century. In the Western Desert of Egypt, for example, various government initiatives have tried to encourage the Bedouin to settle permanently and produce cash crops. While

AL-AZHAR UNIVERSITY

Al-Azhar University in Cairo, Egypt, is one of the most prestigious universities in the Islamic and Arab world. It is named for the daughter of the Prophet Muhammad, Fatima Zahra. The university claims to being the world's oldest seat of learning still in continuous use; the mosque attached to it was founded in 971 and its school of theology dates to 988 (the oldest European universities were only founded in the 12th century). Al-Azhar been a major center of learning for Islamic Law and the Arabic language for centuries. More recently, in the 1960s, it established schools of medicine and engineering. Since the university regards its main role as promoting Islamic religion and culture, only practicing Muslims may attend. Its most senior member, the Grand Imam Sheikh Al-Ahzar, is a very influential figure among Sunni Muslims in the modern world. Al-Ahzar is an example of Egypt's cultural prominence in the Arab world, with a tradition of scholarship that goes back more than one thousand years.

they still manage to retain some aspects of their Bedouin culture, today these groups are not much more nomadic than their settled neighbors.

CULTURE AND RELIGION

The core of Arab identity is formed by devotion to the Islamic faith. Almost all Arabs—regardless of whether they are urban, rural, or nomadic—are practicing Muslims. How they practice their faith depends on the environment in which they live. So, urban populations are able to attend mosque regularly on Fridays for prayer, whereas nomadic populations have to conduct their ritual prayer in a less public and communal setting.

Al-Azhar University in Cairo is regarded by Sunni Muslims as the most prestigious school of Islamic law. Its library contains hundreds of thousands of Arabic books and manuscripts, some dating back to the eighth century.

original Arab invaders. Rather, it is more accurate to say that North African Arabs are made up of a diverse mix of peoples—including the ancient Egyptians, Berbers, and Turks—who all adopted the Muslim faith and later laid claim to Arab identity. Conversely, a more recent trend has been for deprived peoples to reclaim their pre-Arab identity as a way of resisting state oppression. For example, the Kabyles of northern Algeria, who are fiercely opposed to that country's government, strongly promote their Berber identity.

Compared with some other North African cultures, Arab culture is more male dominated, with women largely excluded from public life. Yet the influence of Western ideas under colonial rule challenged traditional attitudes. Egypt was at the forefront of a new Islamic feminist movement, with pioneers like Hoda Sharawi (1879–1947) being the first women to abandon their veils, adopt European dress, and play a more prominent part in public life. At the same time, some women mobilized to oppose these changes, founding groups like the Muslim Sisters in the 1930s.

The role of women has become one of the major battlegrounds between modernists and Islamists in modern North Africa. North Africa has led the Arab world in promoting women's rights, particularly in countries such as Morocco and Tunisia. In 2004, Morocco introduced a new Family Code, providing equal status in marriage for women. This had already been a feature of Tunisian law for some time. Yet in all countries it is generally only wealthier women who have the opportunity and the education to make use of such legal advantages. For poorer women, their legal position often makes little difference to their daily life.

From the point of view of many Arabs, Islam is an essential part of Arab identity. In other words, for many to be Arab is to be a Muslim. The Coptic Christian population of Egypt, for example, speaks Arabic as a first language, is indistinguishable from the Muslim population in terms of physical appearance, and likely has a similar ancestry to their Muslim fellow Egyptians. Yet their Christian faith usually excludes them from Arab identity, and they are generally referred to as Copts, not Arabs.

To reinforce their sense of Arab identity, many North African peoples have embraced traditions that claim they are descended from Arabians. Yet only a tiny proportion of people can truly trace their descent from the

SEE ALSO: Arabic literature; Berbers; Calligraphy; Copts; Festival and ceremony; Islam; Marriage and the family; Oral literature.

ARCHITECTURE

NOTABLE NORTH AFRICAN BUILDINGS

City	Country	Building
Cairo	Egypt	Ibn Tulun Mosque
Cairo	Egypt	Citadel
Kairouan	Tunisia	Great Mosque
Aït Benhaddou	Morocco	*Ksar* (fortified village)
Rabat	Morocco	Chellah (city walls)
Leptis Magna	Libya	Hunting baths/market square
Giza	Egypt	Great Pyramid of Khufu

THE ARCHITECTURE OF NORTH AFRICA HAS BEEN SHAPED BY THE MANY INVADERS WHO SETTLED IN THE REGION, FROM THE PHOENICIANS AND ROMANS TO COLONISTS FROM FRANCE AND ITALY. HOWEVER, THE MOST CHARACTERISTIC BUILDING STYLES ARE THOSE THAT HAVE DEVELOPED UNDER THE INFLUENCE OF ISLAM.

The Great Mosque at Kairouan, Tunisia is built on a rectangular ground plan, measuring some 400 by 240 feet (120 by 73 m). This huge space contains a prayer hall and a courtyard. Inside, the mosque is lavishly decorated in the Islamic style, with ornamentation based on plants and geometric forms and calligraphy (ornamental writing) reproducing verses from the Quran.

PUBLIC ARCHITECTURE

North Africa has a long tradition of public architecture. The ancient Egyptians and Nubians erected monumental buildings, most famously the Pyramids at Giza. Leptis Magna and Cyrene, in Libya, are among the best-preserved ancient Roman sites, together with the originally Phoenician and later Roman city of Carthage in modern Tunisia. There are also well-preserved ruins of Greek settlements in the region.

With the Arab conquest of North Africa came Islamic architecture, including such

KAIROUAN—A KEY CITY

Kairouan (or al-Qayrawan) in northern Tunisia was founded by the Arab military leader Uqba ibn Nafi in 670, on the site of a former fortress of the Byzantine empire. The settlement was intended first and foremost as an *amsar*, or garrison, for the Arab conquest of the Maghreb, which was completed by 711. Thereafter, the city was made the administrative center of the Maghreb under the Aghlabid dynasty, who established an independent emirate over Ifriqiya (Tunisia and eastern Algeria) from 800 onward. The Aghlabids enjoyed a lavish court lifestyle and built a fleet that dominated the central Mediterranean. The magnificent Great Mosque dates from their reign. Kairouan also became a major center of religious learning, and is still regarded as one of the holy cities of Islam.

famous structures as the Cairo citadel— a royal residence and barracks built by the ruler Salah ud-Din (Saladin) in the 12th century and the Great Mosque of Kairouan (seventh–13th centuries). Under the Umayyad caliphate, and later the Abbasids, many innovative buildings were erected in North Africa; the architectural forms adopted there spread to Europe with the Moorish invasion of Spain from the eighth century onward.

Religious architecture in North Africa is typified by the mosque. The towers, or minarets, from which the faithful are called to prayer five times daily, became a common feature of mosques in the ninth century. Today they are one of the distinctive features of the skyline of any Islamic city. Many North African mosques have a square minaret, a style that was later introduced into West Africa.

Non-religious Islamic architecture of past centuries includes the extensive sewage works, aqueducts, and more than 250 reservoirs around Kairouan. These structures display impressive engineering skills; recent archaeological excavations showed them to be the work of the Aghlabid dynasty in the ninth to 10th centuries.

North African cities have certain structural features in common. Many were enclosed by walls that still survive today: for

example the Chellah, the ancient city wall of Rabat (Morocco), is more than 3 miles (5 km) long. The oldest parts of North African cities typically include a medina and a kasbah. The medina is the historic heart of the city, usually a maze of narrow streets, while the kasbah is a walled citadel that provided defense for the city as well as lodgings for the ruling family. Some kasbahs were built on the top of hills, others placed near harbors; the kasbah in Rabat is encircled by walls and gates built in the 16th and 17th centuries on ancient foundations.

Around these historic cores are newer neighborhoods; many North African cities include a European-influenced quarter laid out by French or Italian architects during the colonial period. For example, the Italian fascist government of the 1930s set great store by architecture and urban planning in their colonies, including Libya. They regarded such projects a way of proclaiming Italy's supposed new greatness. Colonial developments typically involved wider, landscaped boulevards laid out on a grid plan, in contrast with the crowded medina. The French modernist architect Le Corbusier pioneered his "machines for living" in the Durand Apartment Project in Algiers.

A Moroccan craftsman making zellige *in the city of Fez. These decorative mosaic tiles are laid out in extremely complex, abstract designs. This art form spread from Fez throughout the Islamic world.*

DOMESTIC ARCHITECTURE

Rural homes, made of mud and stone, are typically rectangular, flat-roofed, and clustered around narrow streets. A less common but striking form of North African domestic architecture is the underground (or troglodyte) dwelling. These houses consist of large pits dug vertically into the ground, from which side chambers are excavated as rooms. The main advantage of these underground houses is that they remain more comfortable than houses above ground in both hot and cold weather. Troglodyte dwellings are found at isolated sites across North Africa, but those of Matmata and Bulla Regia (Tunisia) are the best known. The idea of underground living may go back centuries years in North Africa, but the houses are now gradually falling into disuse as air conditioning and heating make above-ground living more attractive.

Similar to kasbahs, but in a rural context, are *ksars*, or fortified villages. The Ouarzazate region of southern Morocco, on

the fringe of the Sahara, is notable for its *ksars*; one of them, Aït Benhaddou, thought to have been founded in the 11th century, contains six kasbahs and about 50 houses and is a UNESCO World Heritage site. Because *ksars* are typically made of compacted earth mixed with water and straw, they require frequent repair. The only effective way of preserving them is to persuade local villagers to live in them and maintain them on a daily basis.

North African architecture today faces the challenge of growing urbanization. The whole Middle East, which includes North Africa, has the second highest urban growth rate in the world, and by 2020 some 70 percent of the area's population will be urban, according to World Bank estimates.

This means that an extra 86 million people, resulting both from population growth and continuing migration from rural to urban areas, will have to be accommodated. Deterioration of the urban environment, uncontrolled sprawl, and poor access to services and housing are all potential problems.

SEE ALSO: *Arabs; Calligraphy; Contemporary art; Islam.*

REBUILDING AGADIR

An earthquake in 1960 destroyed all but a small quarter of the port of Agadir in Morocco, killing 15,000 people. The authorities saw an opportunity to rebuild the city in a modern Arabic style, and decided to blend European and Arab architectural forms. The Courtyard Houses, a development of single-story row houses, were part of this planned massive reconstruction. Compact, inexpensive to build, and easy to maintain, these houses received great praise and architectural awards. While managing to ensure their occupants' privacy, they were still cool and airy (essential in Morocco's hot climate), thanks to the architects' ingenious use of courtyards and effective ventilation.

The crenellated walls and towers of Aït Benhaddou in Morocco. These magnificent buildings have been used as the location for many movies, including Gladiator.

BAGGARA

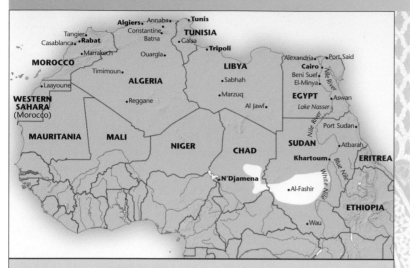

FACT FILE

Population	Approximately 1,000,000 mostly living in western Sudan and eastern Chad.
Religion	Sunni Islam
Language	Most Baggara speak a distinctive local dialect of Arabic. Some groups in Kordofan speak Tama, a Nilo-Saharan language.

TIMELINE

c.975	Bedouins migrate to the Eastern desert in Egypt.
c.1350	Juhayna Bedouin migrate into Nubia and western Sudan.
1570s	Spread of Shuwa Arabs into Darfur and Kordofan along the Sahel corridor as far as Lake Chad.
c.1600	Emergence of the Islamic Sultanate of Darfur.
1821	Kordofan is conquered by the Egyptian Empire.
1856	Al-Zubair, an Egyptian slave trader, establishes a private state in Darfur, with Baggara as middlemen.
1874	Darfur is incorporated into the Egyptian empire.
1881–85	Baggara take part in the Mahdist rebellion. The khalifa ("successor") Abd Allah, a Baggara, becomes leader of the Mahdist state after the death of the Mahdi.
1898	Fall of the Mahdist empire to British forces. The British kill the khalifa in battle and gain control over Sudan.
1956	Sudan wins independence but descends into civil war.
1983	Hostilities resume in Sudan. Baggara peoples form militias and fight against Nilotic pastoralist groups.
1989	Military coup establishes Islamist rule in Sudan.
2003	Darfur crisis begins. Janjaweed, including Baggara militia, carry out attacks on non-Muslim groups.

THE TERM *BAGGARA*—FROM THE ARABIC WORD *BAKAR*, MEANING CATTLE—IS USED TO DESCRIBE A NUMBER OF PASTORALIST GROUPS CONCENTRATED IN CENTRAL SUDAN AND EASTERN CHAD.

HISTORY

The Baggara are thought to descend from the nomadic Juhayna Bedouin of Arabia, who migrated into Africa from the 10th century onward. Settling first in the Eastern desert of Egypt, these peoples undertook a further period of migration in the early 14th century into what is now northern Sudan, settling along the middle stretches of the Nile.

Shuwa Arabs, the probable direct ancestors of the Baggara peoples, spread farther west, establishing themselves in the less arid pasturelands of the western Sudanese provinces of Darfur and Kordofan and throughout the Sahel as far as Lake Chad by the late 16th century. They adopted cattle herding and intermingled with sub-Saharan pastoralists, gradually diverging from other Arab populations over time. They were vassals to the Darfur and Waddai sultanates during the 18th and 19th centuries and were also involved in slave raids on southern non-Muslim peoples throughout the 1800s.

Several Baggara groups took part in the Mahdist uprising (1881–83) against the Egyptians and took up senior positions in the Mahdist state. They were incorporated into the Anglo-Egyptian Condominium that jointly ruled Sudan during the colonial era.

Since independence in 1956, Sudan has been caught up in a recurring civil war. Competition for grazing land between the Baggara and non-Arab pastoralists such as the Dinka has brought ethnic conflict. During the phase of the civil war that began in the early 1980s, many Baggara formed mounted militia groups and attacked non-Muslims. In the Darfur crisis, which began in 2003, these groups (collectively called the Janjaweed) have been involved in the murder and rape of civilians, allegedly encouraged by the Islamist Sudanese government.

SOCIETY AND DAILY LIFE

The Baggara peoples are principally nomadic cattle herders who undertake seasonal migrations south during the dry season to find grazing land, and then north again during the wet season. However, some Baggara live semi-settled lives, keeping two homes at any given time: an impermanent camp and a village house. Camp units are known as *furgan* and consist of a number of related families, each with a male leader known as a sheikh. Millet is widely cultivated to supplement meat and milk; cotton is also grown to be sold at market. Among more sedentary Baggara groups, arable land tends to be individually owned, while grazing land is shared communally.

CULTURE AND RELIGION

Almost all Baggara are Sunni Muslims and strongly maintain their claims to Arabian ancestry and identity. Wealthier individuals often undertake

"BLOOD MONEY" AND THE OMODIYA

Baggara societies are usually subdivided into different sections called *omodiya*, each of which is a lineage that claims descent from a single male ancestor. The *omodiya* play an important part in settling disputes between individuals, by sharing the responsibility for pain or injuries caused. For example, if a man from one *omodiya* kills a man from another, the *omodiya* of the victim is entitled to receive "blood money" in the form of a number of cattle from the *omodiya* of the killer. In this process, all sections of the *omodiya* are expected to contribute when payments are made and are entitled to a share when payments are received.

the hajj (the pilgrimage to Mecca). Their religious practices may incorporate elements from other African peoples, such as belief in the "evil eye" (a form of harmful envy directed either consciously or unconsciously by a living person). Sick children may wear a bracelet or necklace with a pouch containing verses from the Quran to ward off illness.

Most Baggara men have one or two wives and wealth is held by men and inherited patrilineally (i.e. from father to son). Men are responsible for planting crops and herding livestock, while women do the milking and sell goods in the marketplace.

SEE ALSO: Arabs; Dinka; Islam; Nuba.

The Messiriya are a subgroup of the Baggara who live in the Kordofan region of central Sudan. Here, women and children lead the annual migration at the onset of the dry season to find better grazing land for their cattle.

BEJA

FACT FILE

Population	1,900,000 mostly living in northeastern Sudan. Smaller populations of around 200,000 also reside in southern Egypt and Eritrea.
Religion	Islam (Sufism)
Language	To-Bedawiye, spoken by most Beja, is a Northern Cushitic language with some 1,300,000 speakers. Many also speak Arabic such as the Ababda group, while several more southern Beja groups, particularly the Beni Amir, use Tigré.

TIMELINE

260–451	The Beja establish control over part of Upper Egypt.
550–600	Christianity is introduced to the Beja via Nubia.
1150–1300	Islam is widely adopted among the Beja peoples.
1821	Egyptian forces under Mehmet Ali occupy Sudan.
1832	A Beja uprising against Egyptian rule is defeated.
1881	Mahdist revolt begins; several Beja groups take part.
1899	Colonial Anglo-Egyptian rule begins.
1956	Sudan gains independence from the British Empire.
1964	The Beja Congress is formed to promote Beja interests.
1969	Colonel Nimeri takes power in a coup, and suppresses all Beja political activity; Nimeri regime lasts 16 years.
1980s	A major drought kills most Beja livestock.
1989	Islamist government formed after a coup.
1997	The Beja Congress commences low-level military resistance to the pro-Arab regime in Sudan.
2004	The Beja Congress rejects the peace deal that is struck to bring the long Sudanese civil war to a close.

LIVING MAINLY IN THE UPLAND COUNTRY BETWEEN THE RED SEA AND THE NILE AND ATBARAH RIVERS, THE BEJA ARE THOUGHT TO BE THE DESCENDANTS OF PEOPLE WHO HAVE INHABITED THIS AREA SINCE LONG BEFORE THE BEGINNING OF RECORDED HISTORY.

HISTORY

Many Beja adopted Christianity from around the sixth century, through contacts with Nubia. However, by the late 13th century, Islam had become widely established. Throughout the Middle Ages the Beja were well known for acting as guides and protectors of desert caravans, and later for pilgrims undertaking the hajj to Mecca.

Until relatively recent times, attempts to incorporate the Beja into nearby states or empires met with little success. They had a loose allegiance to the Funj sultanate in the 18th and early 19th centuries, and were required to pay tribute to Mehmet Ali's Egyptian empire in the 1840s. Many thousands of Beja died fighting Egyptian forces in the Mahdist revolt of 1881–83.

Under colonialism, the British exercised indirect rule by appointing various local chiefs to administer the Beja. Increased urbanization during the 20th century, such as the building of Port Sudan in the 1920s, saw some Beja abandon their nomadic lifestyle in favor of work as dock laborers.

From the mid-20th century onward the Beja have faced several crises, including loss of livestock as a result of severe droughts in the 1940s and 1980s and loss of grazing land through competition with other groups (many of whom are refugees from nearby conflict zones). Although most Beja are still livestock herders, many now live in urban areas, often in shantytowns. Ethnic tensions have arisen between them and other groups.

SOCIETY AND DAILY LIFE

The Beja have long been a camel-herding people, although some subgroups, notably the Hadandowa, also herd goats and sheep. Many Beja supplement their diet by growing sorghum. Nomadic Beja usually migrate between summer and winter grazing lands throughout the year in small groups of about 8–10 families known as *diwabs*. Authority is usually vested in male heads of extended families, although for the most part Beja societies lack any formal classes or castes.

CULTURE AND RELIGION

Most Beja are Muslims, and belong to brotherhoods such as the Khatmayah sect that follow the mystical form of Islam known as Sufism. Many Beja observe preexisting beliefs alongside their devotion to Islam. Under Islamic Sharia law men are permitted to marry four wives (if all can be treated equally), although in practice only the wealthy do so. Wealth is usually controlled by men and inherited patrilineally (from father to son). When a Beja man marries, his family is expected to pay bridewealth, in the form of livestock, to his wife's kin. Despite the key role of Islamic law, the Beja maintain their own legal traditions—including a system of compensation graded according to the severity of the crime, which is paid by the guilty party to the victim.

Beja men were once known for their distinctive bushy hairstyles, which symbolized their strength and masculinity. Beja women customarily wear their hair long in braids that end in a knot, and daub it with fat. It is taboo for men to perform certain tasks, such as house building or cooking, while women are not allowed to milk livestock. Most groups, except those living on the Red Sea coast, observe a taboo against eating fish.

SEE ALSO: *Arabs; Dinka; Nuba.*

In common with many other groups who live in the Sahara and the Sahel, the Beja build shelters from poles and woven palm matting. These structures are designed to be easy to dismantle and transport.

THE BEJA AND CAMEL HERDING

Livestock play an extremely important part in the daily life of the Beja people. Their camels supply them with meat and milk and also provide transportation. The Beja are celebrated camel breeders, having traded these animals with the peoples of Egypt and Arabia for centuries. Many traditional Beja songs describe the beauty and fineness of their beasts of burden. The three main Beja camel breeds are the Shallagea, Aririt, and Matiaat, which are prized for their milk yield, endurance, and racing prowess respectively. Beja camels are often sold at the Souk Abu Zayd in Khartoum, the largest camel market in Sudan.

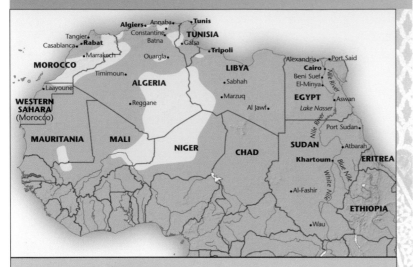

FACT FILE

Population	Main populations: Morocco 7,500,000; Algeria 5,200,000; Libya 169,000
Religion	Muslim
Language	The Berber language (or Tamasheq) are part of the Afro-Asiatic family. Some of the major dialects include Kabyle, spoken by up to 7 million people in Algeria; Tachelhit, spoken by 3 million people in central Morocco; and Tarifit, spoken by some 2 million in northern Morocco.

TIMELINE

3000 B.C.E.	Berbers are settled on the coast of North Africa.
c.250 B.C.E.	Berbers establish three states (Mauretania and two Numidian kingdoms) along North African coast.
8th century	Berbers invade and conquer Spain.
11th century	Banu Hillal invasions strengthen Arab culture and Islam throughout northern Africa.
1086 onward	The Almoravids, a Berber dynasty from Mauretania, conquer Spain and the western half of North Africa. They engage in missionary activity south of the Sahara, promoting the spread of Islam and gaining substantial control over emerging trans-Sahara trade.
1140s–13th century	The Almohads, a Berber dynasty from the Atlas mountains, defeat the Almoravids. They conquer all of northern Africa as well as Spain.
1956	Morocco gains its independence from France.
1962	Algeria attains independence from France.
1994	Berber is accepted as an official language in Algeria and Morocco.
1998, 2000, 2003	Zinedine Zidane, a French citizen of Kabyle Berber origin, is voted the world's best soccer player.

THE BERBERS LIVE MAINLY IN THE ATLAS MOUNTAINS OF MOROCCO AND ALGERIA, WITH SMALLER COMMUNITIES IN THE SAHARA AND SAHEL. THERE ARE MANY DIFFERENT BERBER GROUPS, INCLUDING THE KABYLES OF THE COAST, THE IMAZIGHEN OF CENTRAL MOROCCO, AND THE MZABIS OF THE SAHARA.

HISTORY

Berber populations have lived in northern Africa for millennia, and in historical times have been marked by European, sub-Saharan, and Arabic immigration. The issue of Arab or Berber identity is bitterly contested in modern North Africa, but genetic evidence indicates that most northwest Africans are of Berber origin, including those who consider themselves Arab.

Several thousand years ago the ancient Egyptians mentioned the Berbers, whom they called *Libyans*, as their western neighbors. It is thought that the Roman emperor Septimus Severus (146–211), the early Christian theologian St. Augustine of Hippo (354–430), and the Moroccan traveler Ibn Battuta (1304–69) may have been Berber.

After the ninth century the Berbers became strongly influenced by Arabs. In particular, the Banu Hillal, a group of Yemeni ancestry, played a key role in bringing Islam and Arab culture to North Africa. The Berbers were quick to convert and in turn to spread the Muslim faith, mainly through the Sahara where they had control of trade routes. Many Berbers adopted the Kharijite form of Islam, with its democratic and non-state-building ethos. In the 11th to 13th centuries the Berbers founded powerful dynasties— the Almoravids and Almohads—that united much of North Africa and ruled Spain.

A Berber farmstead high in the Atlas mountains of Morocco. The Berbers mostly live a settled existence, growing cereals and vegetables and herding cattle, sheep, and goats.

Soon after independence in the 1950s and early 1960s, the countries of North Africa identified themselves as Arab nations and established Arabic as their official language. As a result, most Berbers had little opportunity to use their native language.

BERBER HOUSES

Berber houses are square or rectangular, have flat roofs and are made of adobe bricks or stone. The walls are thick, to keep the heat in during the winter and out during the very hot summer. There are few windows for the same reason. Usually built on two floors, the ground floor of a Berber house is a stable in which animals such as cows, goats, and chickens are kept. Above this are the living quarters, comprising a single large room where people eat and sleep. Its floor is covered with many large, colorful carpets, woven locally using sheep's or goat's wool.

In 1963–65 and again in 1980, Berbers in Algeria staged uprisings against the Arab-dominated government. In recent decades Berbers have demanded greater recognition from their governments, and many organizations promote Berber cultural values. Algeria, where the Berber rights movement is particularly strong, has now rewritten its constitution to define itself as an Arab, Berber, and Muslim nation. Despite this tensions continue; Kabylia, for example, is still a hotbed of Berber activism and major antigovernment unrest.

SOCIETY AND DAILY LIFE

Although often romanticized as a nomadic people crossing the Sahara on camels, there are now very few Berbers who follow this lifestyle. Most Berbers are oasis dwellers or settled farmers growing crops on mountains or in valleys. In the past, through their extensive trading networks the Berbers had a major influence on African history. They were middlemen for much of the trans-Saharan trade between North and West Africa, and were key players in the spread of Islam.

Berber society was traditionally divided between those who tended the land and those who did not. At one time, agriculture was considered the work of the lower classes, while the upper classes were merchants. Over time, these distinctions have faded; some settled farmers have become wealthy or been given political status by colonial and independent administrations, while trans-Saharan trade has lost its importance.

CULTURE AND RELIGION

Berbers are predominantly Muslim; accordingly, the festivals that they celebrate are those associated with Islam, such as Eid ul-Fitr and Eid ul-Kebir (see ISLAM).

The Berbers excel in making jewelry, pottery, leather, and finely woven carpets. Berber art has a high reputation and tour

OTHMANE BALI

Othmane Bali (1953–2005), from Djanet in the Algerian Sahara, was a Berber musician who introduced *tindé*, the musical style of his home region, to a wider public. Trained as a medical doctor, Othmane Bali was best known for his lute playing and singing in Tamasheq, Arabic, and French. He performed Berber music in festivals and concerts around the world, with his relatives, including his mother Khadidjata, as backing singers. Passionate about his art, Bali described his role in the following terms: "I sing of Algeria, the Muslim world, the love of the desert. . . I want to revive our roots, which are our reason to live. A tree without roots will not grow." He also fused *tindé* with other musical traditions, producing three albums with the Cherokee-Irish artist Steve Shehan and performing his last show with French jazzman Jean-Marc Padovani. Bali died in June 2005 when a flash flood swept away his car in Djanet.

operators include a visit to a Berber market among the attractions of a North African trip. Women of the Irifiyen group in northeastern Morocco are known especially for their decorated pottery. Traditional blue and white glazes, which first became common with the spread of Islam, are used to highlight geometric motifs on pottery. Much of the woolen carpet and blanket production of Morocco is in the hands of Berbers from the Atlas mountains. Each village has its own distinctive weaving technique, geometric designs, and color combinations. A wide variety of silver jewelry is made; the Souss area of Tunisia is noted for the Berber silver jewelry produced there. Brass or silver trays and pots are also well known.

SEE ALSO: *Arabs; Baggara; Islam; Metalwork; Textiles.*

Berber riders perform in a fantasia *(an equestrian pageant) in Marrakech, Morocco. Berbers have long been renowned for their horsemanship since ancient times.*

THE HAND OF FATIMA

Among the silver jewelry made by the Berbers, a famous motif is the "Hand of Fatima," named for the daughter of the Prophet Muhammad, Fatima Zahra, a role-model for women. Also known by the Arabic name *khamsa* (meaning "five"), this flat amulet in a stylized hand shape symbolizes the core principles of the Muslim faith—the Five Pillars of Islam. The *khamsa* is thus thought to protect its wearer from the "evil eye," a form of harmful envy directed consciously or unconsciously by a living person. The same shape is also used for door knockers to ward off evil spirits from the home.

Wearing the robes and silver jewelry of a prospective bride, a young Berber girl takes part in a mass engagement festival in Morocco. Berber girls generally marry at the age of 15 or 16, and follow the common Muslim practice of an arranged marriage.

CALLIGRAPHY

ISLAM IN ITS STRICTEST FORM BANS THE REPRESENTATION IN ART OF HUMANS AND OTHER LIVING THINGS. THIS IS SEEN AS AN ARROGANT CHALLENGE TO ALLAH'S CREATIVE SUPREMACY. INSTEAD, ISLAMIC ART FOCUSES ON GEOMETRIC DESIGNS AND ELABORATE, DECORATIVE SCRIPTS OF RELIGIOUS TEXTS KNOWN AS CALLIGRAPHY. FROM TEXTILES TO STONEWORK AND WOODCARVINGS, CALLIGRAPHY IS FOUND WIDELY ACROSS THE ISLAMIC WORLD.

HISTORY

Muslims believe that the holiness of the Quran lends a special aura to the written word. Accordingly, since its beginnings, Islam has placed great emphasis on elaborate textual decoration. When the prophet Muhammad died in 632 his disciples urged his successors, the first caliphs, to set down in writing the Quran—the Recitation of the Word of Allah, revealed to Muhammad by the angel Jibril (Gabriel). Thus a tradition of scribes and ornate scripts was born. The first master calligrapher was Abu Ali Muhammad Ibn Muqlah in Baghdad in the early 10th century, who devised a standardized script to simplify correspondence and record keeping in the Abbasid caliphate. His work was elaborated by Ibn al-Bawwab in the 11th century and Yaqut al-Mustasimi in the late 13th century. Together, these three masters are credited with the creation of the modern scripts.

The oldest form of Arabic calligraphy is Kufic, which was in use on the Arabian peninsula before the advent of Islam. This is the script in which the first copies of the Quran were made. Over time, distinctive types of Kufic script developed in the Arabian peninsula (Eastern Kufic) and in the Maghreb (Western Kufic). Further styles were then created for writing in books and for use on monumental inscriptions. These included the cursive Naskh script for use in casual writing, the beautifully clear Riqa script, which is known for its straight lines and readability, and the highly ornamental Thuluth script. Thuluth was used widely from the 13th century onward for decorative architectural inscriptions in mosques.

As Islam spread eastward through the Arab conquest of the Persian Sasanian empire, the Persians adopted Arabic script for writing their own language. Two distinctive calligraphic styles grew up there—Taliq and Nastaliq, characterized by long, horizontal strokes. Finally, in the 16th and 17th centuries, the Diwani style was developed in the Turlish Ottoman empire.

In the past written calligraphy employed a variety of tools including reed and brush pens, a knife for cutting the pens and an ink pot with various inks. The reed pen (*qalam*) remains the most important tool of the calligrapher and great care must be taken over selecting and maintaining these pens. Ink came in many colors including black, brown, white, red, yellow, blue, silver, and gold and the recipes for making them were closely guarded secrets. Paper was mostly made from cotton or silk but rarely from wood pulp. As well as copying extracts from the Quran, many calligraphers developed their own compositions and those of the great masters have been copied time and again throughout the Islamic world.

CALLIGRAPHY IN NORTH AFRICA

In Egypt the arts were championed under the Mamluke sultanate (1260–1517) and calligraphy was widely practiced. Objects such as lamps, glass, candlesticks, manuscripts, and wooden minbars (pulpits) were decorated with calligraphy and many works are regarded as exemplary

A Muslim places his hand on the word Allah *carved in stone on the facade of the Bou Inania Medersa, a former Quranic college in Morocco. This inscription is written in the Tuluth calligraphic style, which was developed from the 11th century onward.*

THE ARABIC ALPHABET

The Arabic language is written from right to left. There are 18 basic letter shapes, which vary depending on whether they are connected to a letter before or after them. The full alphabet of 29 letters is created by placing various dots and dashes above or below the basic letter shapes. Although the Arabic alphabet that we know today appears highly distinctive, it is actually very closely related to the alphabets used in ancient Greek, Phoenician, and Aramaic (an ancient Near Eastern language), from which Latin later derived. The numerals used throughout the Western world (1, 2, 3, 4. . . . etc) were originally Arabic, and were adopted because they offered significant mathematical advantages over the relatively clumsy Roman numeral system (that is I, II, III, IV. . . . etc).

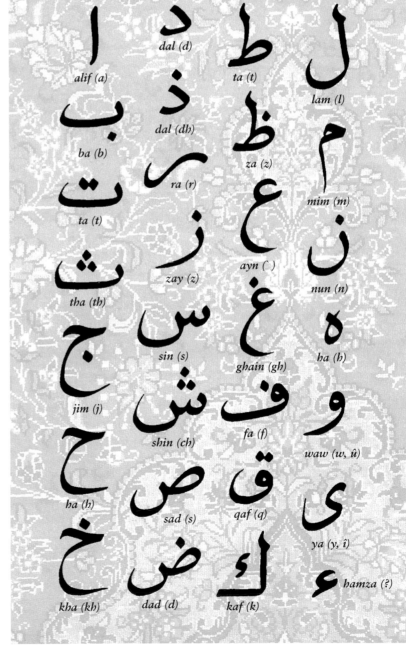

masterpieces. There were numerous Mamluke master calligraphers, including Muhammad Ibn al-Wahid and Muhammad Ibn Sulayman al-Muhsini.

An interesting style of calligraphy to emerge in North Africa during the 20th century was that of the Khartoum school. Developed at the Faculty of Fine and Applied Art at the Sudan University of Technology, this style is characterized by its ingenious blending of Arabic and African forms, expressing the dual African and Islamic identity of Sudan.

See Also: Arabic literature; Arabs; Architecture; Islam; Leatherwork; Metalwork.

CHRISTIANITY

TIMELINE

c.55–68 St. Mark is said to have introduced Christianity to Egypt and is martyred in Alexandria.

313–91 Roman Emperor Constantine and his successors allow Christianity; paganism banned by Theodosius I.

451 The Coptic Church splits from the Catholic and Orthodox churches at the Council of Chalcedon.

641 onward Arab armies overrun North Africa; Christians are tolerated as "People of the Book."

1250–1517 Christianity ceases to be the dominant faith in Egypt. Egypt's Muslim rulers occasionally persecute Christians.

1989 Sudan imposes Islamic law; the Christian south rebels.

1990s Islamist extremists attack Coptic targets in Egypt.

CHRISTIANITY ARRIVED IN NORTH AFRICA IN THE FIRST CENTURY AND GAINED GROUND AFTER THE ROMAN EMPIRE BECAME OFFICIALLY CHRISTIAN. WHEN ISLAM SPREAD ACROSS THE REGION IN THE SEVENTH AND EIGHTH CENTURIES, CHRISTIANS WERE ALLOWED TO KEEP THEIR FAITH. HOWEVER, OVER TIME THEIR NUMBERS HAVE DWINDLED, AND ONLY SOUTHERN SUDAN NOW HAS A MAJORITY CHRISTIAN POPULATION.

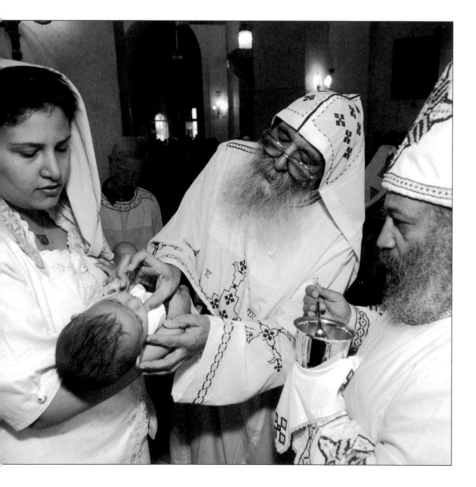

Coptic priests bless a baby during a church service in Bilyana, Egypt. The Egyptian Coptic Church is now more than 19 centuries old, and there are thought to be some 8 million Copts in the country.

EARLY HISTORY

The evangelist St. Mark is said to have brought Christianity to Egypt soon after Jesus was crucified. The faith quickly took root there, and also spread westward into other parts of Roman North Africa. Egypt, in particular, was central to the development of Christian ideas: important early North African Christian thinkers and teachers include St. Cyril (d. 444), St. Athanasius (296–373), and St. Augustine of Hippo (354–430). The idea of religious orders of monks living a life of prayer and devotion apart from society was first developed in late Roman times by the founding fathers of the Egyptian Coptic Church.

SPREAD AND CONTRACTION

After the Roman empire had persecuted Christians for centuries, the emperor Theodosius I (347–95) made Christianity the official religion of Rome in 391. This naturally helped strengthen its position in the empire's North African provinces. Yet it also meant that any forms of worship or belief that did not match those of the ruling emperor or church leaders were brutally suppressed. This had particularly serious consequences in Egypt, where fundamental

invaded Egypt in 641 and defeated the country's Byzantine overlords.

Farther west along the North African coast—the region known as the Maghreb—Christianity suffered greatly from the collapse of the Roman empire and invasion by the Vandals from 442. Cities such as Carthage and Hippo Regius that had been Christian strongholds were sacked. Yet several Christianized Berber kingdoms survived in areas beyond the limits of Roman rule.

Following the Arab conquest of the Maghreb at the beginning of the eighth century, Christianity survived, but in ever-dwindling communities, finally disappearing around 1200. In Egypt, on the other hand, where Christianity was more deeply embedded in national life, the Coptic Church continued to thrive. The Copts only began to be outnumbered by Muslims in the 13th century. Since medieval times, the Copts have been subject to several periods of persecution, often because they traditionally occupied high-ranking posts and enjoyed above-average prosperity. Under Mamluke rule (1250–1517) for example, Copts were sometimes harassed and their churches closed; this was echoed in more recent times, when the Arab nationalism that swept Egypt after independence (from 1952 onward) saw Copts dismissed from their official posts. Yet Coptic Christianity clung on, and even today many millions of Egyptians still belong to the Coptic Church.

From the sixth century until as late as 1700 Coptic Christianity also flourished farther south; numerous churches and monasteries have been discovered and excavated by archaeologists in Nubia. But because Christianity was closely linked to the political elites of the Nubian kingdoms, it did not survive the destruction of those states by new Muslim rulers.

differences in belief arose between the local Coptic Church and the Orthodox Church, the official religion of the Eastern Roman Empire that ruled the region (see COPTS). Consequently, the country's Coptic majority warmly welcomed the Arab armies that

The Eastern Orthodox monastery of St. Catherine (527–65) lies below Mt. Sinai, where God gave Moses the Ten Commandments.

MODERN CONVERSIONS

Alongside the Coptic Church of Egypt, there are a number of other Christian denominations in North Africa. Some, such as the Greek Orthodox and Armenian communities of Egypt, have roots that are several centuries old, while others are a product of European colonialism. More recent forms of Christianity are especially active in Sudan, where many black Africans living in the south of the country converted under (and since) British rule. Their rejection of Islamic Sharia law and Arab domination fueled Sudan's long-running, civil wars (1955–73 and 1983–2004). Although most Sudanese Christians are Anglicans or Roman Catholics, evangelical Protestant churches are also attracting growing numbers of converts there.

SEE ALSO: *Arabs; Copts; Dinka; Festival and ceremony; Islam; Nubians; Nuer.*

ARTISTS IN NORTH AFRICA

Artist	Dates	Country	Style/Medium
Gazbiah Sirry	b.1925	Egypt	Painting
Baya Mahieddine	1931–99	Algeria	Painting
Farid Belkahia	b.1934	Morocco	Natural multimedia (dyes, pottery, handmade paper, lambskins)
Rachid Koraïchi	b.1947	Algeria	Multimedia, installation
Gouider Triki	b.1949	Tunisia	Engraving
Hassan Musa	b.1951	Sudan	Illustration, performance art
Fatma Charfi	b.1955	Tunisia	Multimedia
Fathi Hassan	b.1957	Egypt/Sudan	Painting
Susan Hefuna	b.1962	Egypt/Germany	Digital photography and video installation
Zineb Sedira	b.1963	Algeria	Video stills and video installation
Ghada Amer	b.1963	Egypt	Painting, sculpture, textiles, installation
Ymane Fakhir	b.1969	Morocco	Photography
Mounir Fatmi	b.1970	Morocco	Stencils, installation, movies

THE TENSION BETWEEN TRADITION AND MODERNITY IS A RECURRENT THEME IN THE CONTEMPORARY ART OF NORTH AFRICA. MANY ARTISTS HAVE TAKEN WESTERN INFLUENCES AND BLENDED THEM WITH LOCAL STYLES TO PRODUCE A DISTINCTIVE AND UNIQUE FUSION.

The indigenous artistic traditions of North Africa are both ancient and varied, ranging from Stone Age rock paintings to the intricate designs and ornamentation of pre-Islamic Berber groups throughout the Maghreb (Morocco, Algeria, Tunisia, and Libya). Following the Arab conquests and the introduction of Islam to the region in the seventh and early eighth centuries, however, many North African countries came under the control of a succession of conquering powers. The Sudanese, for example, were first invaded by Bedouin Arabs in the 1300s and later became the colonial subjects of first Ottoman (Turkish) and then Anglo-Egyptian rulers.

North Africa, then, has been subject to many centuries of outside influence, and many foreign powers have imposed their ideas of nationality and identity on its peoples. Perhaps for this reason, a major concern of contemporary North African artists is to question the whole meaning of nationhood and collective identity. In some countries, colonialism and the wars resulting from it have caused populations to split along ethnic, linguistic, cultural, and religious lines. In such circumstances, a powerful tension has arisen between an identity that is associated with indigenous

A striking form of official art in the Arab world is the billboard or mural glorifying a national figure. Here, a huge painting of Libyan leader Muammar Qaddafi stands outside the city of Sirte.

culture, and a more recent identity that is associated with the state. It is these tensions that modern artists often attempt to capture and explore in their work.

WESTERN INFLUENCES

There is another tension evident in the work of North Africa's contemporary artists that relates to matters of style. This tension is between art forms and styles that are regarded as indigenous and those that have been adopted from Western art. Many North African art movements were influenced by European trends and styles. For example, the founding members of the Moroccan Casablanca School, established in the early 1960s, all attended the Ecole des Beaux-Arts in Paris, where they became aware of early 20th-century Modernism.

In Egypt, from as early as the 1930s, the first generation of modern artists innovated

and experimented with the avant-garde European styles of the period, such as Surrealism, Cubism, and Dadaism. These artists also became politically engaged, founding the Egyptian Art and Freedom Group in 1939. In the face of much criticism, its members argued that European art posed no threat to Egyptian national

Moroccan women walk past a colorful mural depicting Muslim women. The mural shows the influence of the modernist Western painter Picasso, who was himself influenced by African sculpture.

GLASS BLOWING: CONTEMPORARY FORMS AND ANCIENT TECHNIQUES

The Tunisian artist Sadika Kammoun (b.1961) revived a Tunisian art form that had not been practiced since the 14th century. After studying for a master's degree at the Académie des Beaux-Arts in Tunis, Kammoun was apprenticed to the artist Gianni Seguso on the famous glassmaking island of Murano near Venice, Italy. Kammoun's work gives traditional domestic household objects a contemporary flair, using bright colors and varied textures and materials. One of her most famous pieces, made for a hotel on the Tunisian island of Djerba, earned her a place in the Guinness Book of Records for the world's largest chandelier.

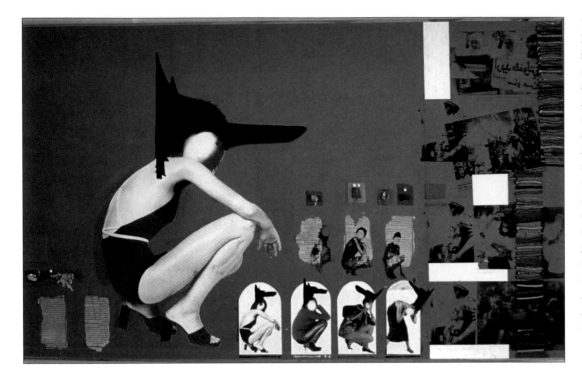

The picture Anubis, Batman, and Other Gods in Downward Motion *(mixed media, 2003) by the Egyptian artist Khaled Hafez (b.1963) is a good example of how contemporary North African artists mix ancient motifs (Anubis was an ancient Egyptian god of the dead) and modern imagery. Hafez won a prize for another work in this series at the Sixth Biennale of African Contemporary Art in Dakar, Senegal, in 2004.*

identity. They therefore called for modern Egyptian art to engage with global concerns as well as being aware of its local heritage. This group also placed great emphasis on personal creativity and the freedom of the individual to express himself or herself through his or her art.

The early 1940s saw the emergence of the Rejectionists, who challenged the romanticized notions of European art that their predecessors had promoted. This set the scene for artists of the Contemporary Art Group (for example the painter Gazbiah Sirry), who from 1946 on turned once more to European art for inspiration, but this time viewed it with a more critical eye. This group focused especially on the contemporary work of the Abstract Expressionists, such as Jackson Pollock.

FUSION OF STYLES

In Sudan throughout the 1950s, the Khartoum School sent all of its most talented art students to London's finest art schools. Many returned to the Khartoum School as teachers, and over time they developed a unique artistic approach that used European techniques to explore Sudan's cultural heritage. These artists reworked elements of folklore and calligraphy into modern compositions in paint and print, and even (in the case of artist Hassan Musa) performance art.

From the mid-20th century many techniques and forms were brought together in works of art that fused local and foreign styles. The Moroccan artist Ahmed Cherkaoui (1934–67), combined classic Berber patterning and motif with colorful abstract shapes and symbols in a subtle blending of Moroccan and European styles. Similarly the Algerian artist Baya Mahieddine (1931–99) used imagery

(Right) A tapestry entitled Desert Landscape, *by the Egyptian artist Ali Selim (b.1946). This artist is one of a number of weavers who have graduated from the Ramses Wissa Wassef Art School near Giza, which specializes in teaching tapestry-making techniques.*

THE OPEN STUDIO PROJECT 2006
The Open Studio Project, which takes place in Cairo, Egypt, is a two-week program for international artists hosted by the Townhouse Gallery of Contemporary Art. The gallery invites 20 artists who work in digital media and sound to take up a two-week residency there. During their stay, they are free to explore, innovate, and collaborate, engaging with one another in a "live" artistic process.

that was based on folklore but which also recalled the dreamlike quality found in the work of European Surrealist painters such as Salvador Dali and Giorgio de Chirico. Another Algerian artist, Rachid Koraïchi (b.1947), who trained at the Ecole de Beaux-Arts, explored the mysticism and symbolism of numbers associated with the ancient, mystical form of Islam called Sufism. Using mixed media (paint, ceramics, textiles, metals, installation, and printmaking) Koraïchi collaborated with local artisans to produce art that is decidedly modern yet which also reflects an ancient heritage.

SEE ALSO: Calligraphy; Festival and ceremony; Islam; Metalwork; Sculpture; Textiles.

SHATAT: ARAB DIASPORA WOMEN ARTISTS

The SHATAT exhibition, held at the University of Colorado in 2003, aimed to examine the role of women in Arab societies. Four female artists, three of them from North Africa, took part in this exploration of gender and the representation of the female body in Muslim society and the wider world. A major theme of the exhibition (whose title means *diaspora* or "scattering" in Arabic) was "reclaiming the female body"—that is, stripping away stereotypes that depict Arab women as obedient and passive. Using installations, performance, and sculpture, the Tunisian artist Fatma Charfi (b.1955) expressed the alienation she feels as a North African woman living in Europe. Susan Hefuna (b.1962), of Egyptian and German parents, used photography and video footage to examine her own mixed identity. The Algerian artist Zineb Sedira (b.1963) uses a traditionally male art form of Arabesque ceramic tiling in her installation *Quatre Générations de Femmes* ("Four Generations of Women"), which explored the gender roles imposed by her society.

COPTS

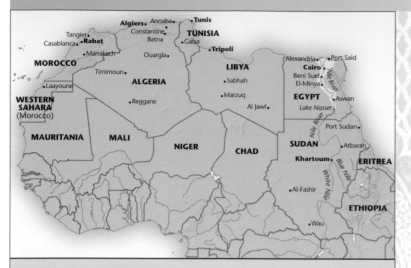

FACT FILE

Population	Estimated at 8 million, all in Egypt.
Religion	Coptic Orthodox Christianity
Language	Arabic (Coptic is only used in church services).

TIMELINE

c.60	Christianity established in Egypt by St. Mark.
200s	Alexandria becomes a major center of worship; first Christian texts in Coptic are written.
284	Major Roman persecution of Christians—the Era of Martyrs—marks the start of the Coptic calendar. Many Christians flee into the desert, where St. Anthony and St. Pachomius found the first monasteries.
391	Christianity made official religion of the Roman Empire.
451	The Coptic Church is founded over doctrinal split at the Council of Chalcedon.
641	Arabs conquer Egypt.
1008–21	Persecution of Christians by Fatimid Caliph al-Hakim.
c.1400	Most Egyptians are now Arabic speaking and Muslim.
c.1700	Coptic language no longer in daily use in Egypt.
1855–56	Hamayouni Decree by Ottoman (Turkish) rulers of Egypt tries to create equality between Muslims and Copts; the "poll tax" on non-Muslims is abolished.
1971	Shenouda III is elected as Coptic Pope and Patriarch of Alexandria.
1981–85	Coptic Pope under house arrest, accused of being a political leader.
1990s	Sporadic terrorist attacks on Coptic targets, especially in central Egypt, carried out by extreme Islamists.

THE COPTS ARE DESCENDED FROM ANCIENT EGYPTIANS WHO CONVERTED TO CHRISTIANITY LONG BEFORE ISLAM CAME TO THE REGION. IN RECENT TIMES, MANY COPTS HAVE SUFFERED PERSECUTION BY THE STATE AND PHYSICAL ATTACKS BY EXTREMISTS.

HISTORY

The term *Copt* comes from the Greek *Aegyptos*, meaning "Egypt." The Coptic Orthodox Church has a distinctive history that reaches back to the early development of Christianity in Egypt. Many of its rituals and observances recall ancient Egyptian practices. These include its calendar, the custom of leaving food offerings for the dead, and visits at New Year to family graves. The shape of the Coptic Cross also comes from the Ancient Egyptian ankh hieroglyph symbolizing life.

The Coptic Church long ago broke away from the other branches of the early Christian Church (which were based in Rome and Constantinople) over the fundamental question of the nature of Jesus Christ. In 451, at the Council of Chalcedon, the Christian Church tried to standardize its doctrine. Both the Eastern Orthodox and the Western (Catholic) churches declared their belief that Jesus Christ has separate divine and human natures. Yet the Coptic Church stressed the unity of the human and divine in the figure of Christ; this belief is known as the Monophysite doctrine.

When Constantinople (the Eastern Roman or Byzantine empire) ruled Egypt in the fourth to seventh centuries, Coptic Christianity took on a nationalistic aspect, becoming the focus of resistance to Byzantine oppression. Consequently, the Coptic majority in Egypt did not resist the Arab Muslim conquest of the region in 641.

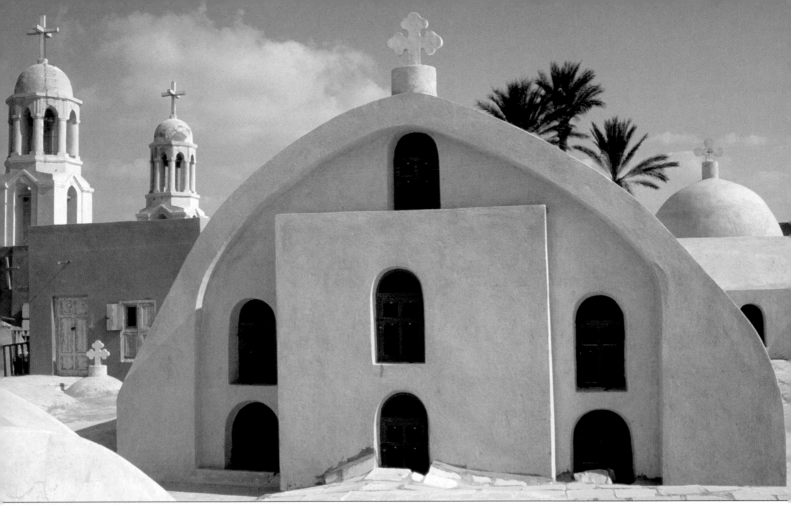

Under Islamic rule the Copts were allowed to continue practicing their religion, though they were subject to some restrictions and higher taxation. Not until the 13th century did they cease to be an absolute majority of the Egyptian population. Even thereafter they continued to play an active part at all levels of Egyptian society.

The early Copts were renowned for their religious art, which took the form of carvings, textiles, and beautifully decorated and bound manuscripts.

A Coptic church at Deir-al-Baramus in Egypt. The Coptic Church is based on the teachings of St. Mark, who introduced Christianity to Egypt in c.60 C.E., and was martyred at Alexandria.

COPTS IN MODERN EGYPT

Today, the Coptic language is only spoken in Coptic church services. Derived directly from ancient Egyptian, Coptic has a large body of literature, mostly on religious subjects. Its written form is based on the Greek alphabet. The language was once widespread but over time gradually disappeared from daily use.

The Copts were historically associated with commerce, banking, and the civil service. Yet with the rise of Arab nationalism in the 1950s, many lost their jobs when their businesses were nationalized. Since 1971, the Coptic Church has seen a revival under Pope Shenouda III. Its monasteries are filled with highly educated monks and nuns, and its churches are focal points for community life. However, in the 1990s Copts and their churches came under attack from extremists. Many Copts emigrated, mainly to the United States, and new dioceses were created there, covering the Southern United States, and Southern California and Hawaii.

THE COPTIC LEGACY: MONASTICISM

One of the Copts' most important contributions to Christianity is the practice of monasticism. In Egypt, the first Christian monks sought refuge in the desert from Roman persecution and the temptations of normal society as early as the middle of the third century. They were inspired to join together in a group by the Coptic hermit St. Anthony of Egypt (c.251–356). His successor Pachomius (290–346) organized the first formal communities with joint meals, worship, and work. From these beginnings, the idea of the monastic life spread through the Christian world. Today Egypt's Coptic monasteries remain important centers of research, learning and pilgrimage.

SEE ALSO: Arabs; Christianity; Islam.

DANCE AND SONG

SINGERS AND COMPOSERS

Singer/Artist	Country	Style
Umm Kulthum	Egypt	Arab Classical
Mohammed abd el-Wahaab	Egypt	Arab Classical
Abd el-Halim Hafez,	Egypt	Arab Classical
Warda Al-Jazairia	Algeria	Arab Classical
Al-Thami Lamdaghri (composer)	Morocco	Milhun
Salah el-Mahdi (composer of the Tunisian national anthem)	Tunisia	Malouf
Albert Bouhadana	Morocco	Sephardic song
Françoise Atlan	Morocco	Sephardic song

The Haissawa dance troupe from Morocco acknowledge applause after their performance at the 2004 Sacred Dance festival at Thies, Senegal.

DANCE AND SONG IN NORTH AFRICA HAVE BEEN HEAVILY INFLUENCED BY ISLAM AND ARAB MIGRATIONS FROM THE SEVENTH CENTURY ONWARD. THE REGION BOASTS A COLORFUL VARIETY OF SONG AND DANCE FORMS.

CLASSICAL ARAB SINGING

In Arab culture poetry has always been considered the noblest of all art forms. As a result, many of the songs of the medieval Arab world were musical settings of famous poems, and this tradition has formed the basis of Arab Classical music. The 20th century produced several superstars in this style, who achieved great fame throughout North Africa. The most famous, even today, is the Egyptian Umm Kulthum (1904–75), who had a repertoire of hundreds of songs and was known for her melancholy operettas that could last for up to an hour. Her live radio broadcasts in the 1950s and 1960s were heavily promoted by the Egyptian government. President Nasser saw her patriotic singing as a way of promoting Arab nationalism.

Similarly the Maghreb has a long-established tradition of song that has its origins in Qasidah, the medieval poetry of al-Andalus (Muslim Spain). The main regional variants of this style are Malouf (Tunisia), Aaroubi (Algeria), and Milhun (Morocco). "Sanaa," the sung element of Andalusi music deals with a variety of themes including religious and secular subjects. Today Andalusi music attracts a wide audience, mainly through television broadcasts, particularly during the Muslim holy month of Ramadan.

Young Berber girls from Algeria perform a dance. Berbers have a rich dance tradition, including the Ahaidous and Ahoauch dances of the Atlas region, and the Guedra dance of southern Morocco.

SONG AND DANCE IN RELIGIOUS CONTEXTS

Although much song that has been produced in the Muslim world has a religious content, mainstream Islam does not incorporate singing or dancing into its formal religious observances, with Friday services in mosques lacking anything that is equivalent to Christian hymns or praise music. Islam has often regarded dancing and singing as

UMM KULTHUM

Umm Kulthum was born into a poor family in rural Egypt. Because she showed a remarkable talent for singing from an early age, her father, the local imam, taught her to chant from the Quran. When she was 12 her father disguised her as a boy so that she could sing in the small choir he conducted. By her early twenties, Kulthum's growing popularity attracted the interest of many artists and politicians including the poet Ahmed Rami (who became her songwriter) and Gamal Abdel Nasser, the future president of Egypt. Umm Kulthum's monthly concerts were broadcast nationwide and during her career she recorded more than 300 songs, the most famous of which were "Al-Atlal," "Inta umri," and "Fakarouni." In 1967 she fell seriously ill and died in Cairo eight years later, on February 3, 1975. The record 4 million mourners who attended her funeral reflected her widespread popularity.

encouraging lustfulness and other forms of immorality. In particular, the idea of women dancing in public was a violation of the principle that they should be secluded and restricted to the private realm of the home and family. Even today many Muslim societies disapprove of dance and song.

The Sufi brotherhoods, found among pastoralists across North Africa, are an exception to this general rule. This mystical branch of Islam relies heavily on song and dance as essential elements of the religious experience. Sufis are best known for their "whirling dervishes," dancers who spin in a circular motion, gradually gaining in speed until they reach a trancelike state of heightened religious awareness. In Sudan such dances are regarded as un-Islamic by the National Islamic Front government, which has tried to discourage them.

Other Islamic peoples such as the Berbers still maintain very old folk-dancing traditions, such as the elaborate Ahaidous (involving men and women) and Ahouach (women only) dances of the High Atlas mountains. Both of these dances involve chanted prayers and take place in the open air within a large ring of spectators. Berber song and dance often form an integral part of festivals (moussems), important ceremonies such as weddings, and seasonal rituals. They are thought to bring protection from misfortune and from the evil spirits known as djinn.

SONGS OF THE SEPHARDIC JEWS

North Africa's Jewish population, which has now largely disappeared after large-scale migration to Israel in the second half of the 20th century, has its own vibrant song tradition. The songs of the Sephardim—Jews who were driven out of Spain in 1492 and emigrated to North Africa and elsewhere—were mostly performed in medieval Spanish and covered a wide range of different themes. Some Sephardic songs dealt with love, such as the well-known romance called the "Gerineldo," while others had a religious content. The songs were usually sung by women without any instrumental accompaniment. A number of modern singers who grew up in this tradition have risen to international prominence including the Moroccans Françoise Atlan, Albert Bouhadana, and Emil Zirhan. Sephardic music is regularly performed at the Festival of Sacred Music, an annual event that takes place in Fez, Morocco, during late spring.

Religious forms of singing and dancing also exist among the non-Muslim peoples of North Africa. The Coptic Christians of Egypt sing hymns set in the Coptic language during their church services (the only situation in which this ancient language is now used). Many musical scholars believe that these Coptic hymns are the last surviving offshoot of ancient Egyptian religious music. Peoples of the southern Sudan for whom cattle are of major social and symbolic importance, such as the Dinka, sing hymns to their livestock while leaping up and down in energetic dances.

SEE ALSO: *Arabs; Berbers; Festival and ceremony; Music and musical instruments; Oral literature.*

THE GUEDRA DANCE OF MOROCCO

The Guedra, or "Dance of Love," is a traditional dance among the Berbers of southern Morocco. It is performed at major festivals, such as the Goulmime Moussem, an annual camel market. The dance is accompanied by folk songs in the medieval Hassani dialect of Arabic, which describe the ancient trials of the Berbers and their migrations through the harsh desert climate. The dance is performed by troupes of up to 17 women for a male audience. At the beginning of the Guedra, the women wear a richly colored indigo veil and for most of the dance only the hands and forearms, decorated with henna body art, are visible as they trace a series of complex and sensuous movements in the air. The final stage of the dance involves the participant throwing off her veil and swinging her hair from side to side, which is elaborately decorated with colored beads.

Mystics who follow the form of Islam known as Sufism are renowned for their "whirling dervish" dances, during which they can enter a trancelike state. Here, Egyptian Sufis perform the Tannura dance at the mausoleum of Sultan Al-Ghuri in Cairo.

FACT FILE

Population	3.2 million, in southern Sudan.
Religion	Christianity, Dinka
Language	Nilotic, a branch of the Nilo-Saharan language family, has three major divisions: Eastern (Plains); Western (River–Lake); and Southern (Highland). Dinka is a Western Nilotic language, closely related to Nuer.

TIMELINE

3000–2000 B.C.E.	Cattle-keeping people speaking an early form of Western Nilotic are resident in southern Sudan.
c.1000 C.E.	Nilotic peoples settle in the region the the far southwest of Bahr al Ghazal river.
1500s	Dinka settled in present location. Different Dinka groups begin to emerge.
1800	Arab slave traders expand into southern Sudan.
1818–90	Nuer expand east of the Nile to the Ethiopian border.
1870–79	British annex Upper Nile and wipe out the slave trade.
1881–89	Islamic Mahdist revolution against British rule.
1920s–1930s	Dinka and Nuer partitioned under British rule.
1920s	Christian missionary schools established in Dinkaland.
1956	Sudanese independence.
1962–72	First Sudanese civil war.
1983	Sharia (Islamic Law) imposed by Khartoum government, sparking the second Sudanese civil war.
1991	Nuer–Dinka split in the Sudanese People's Liberation Army (SPLA).
2005	SPLA leader John Garang signs peace accord with Khartoum government, and is appointed vice-president, but dies in a helicopter crash.

THE DINKA ARE A NILOTIC PEOPLE WHO HISTORICALLY INHABITED A VAST ARC AROUND THE SWAMPS OF THE UPPER NILE BASIN IN SOUTHERN SUDAN. THEY MAKE UP THE LARGEST ETHNIC GROUP IN SUDAN, BUT HAVE LONG STRUGGLED TO ASSERT THEIR RIGHTS AGAINST THE ISLAMIC, ARAB CULTURE OF THE NORTH.

HISTORY

Despite the large numbers of Dinka inhabiting the Upper Nile region, oral history and written records both tell of a massive territorial expansion in the 19th century by their neighbors the Nuer, largely at the Dinka's expense. The Dinka comprise around 25 self-governing territorial groupings that enjoy a common culture. However, they have never been politically unified, and so were unable to put up an effective resistance against the Nuer. Since the early 1960s, the Dinka have been heavily involved in Sudan's civil wars, with the Sudanese People's Liberation Army (SPLA) being led by a Dinka, John Garang. In 2005 the Sudanese civil war ended with the southern rebels being incorporated into the Khartoum government; however, Garang was killed in a helicopter crash just three weeks after being appointed vice-president.

SOCIETY AND DAILY LIFE

Over the past two centuries, Dinka culture has shown itself able to adapt and adjust to many different external influences. In particular, the period of British rule

Dinka women prepare sorghum at a village in southern Sudan. This staple cereal is first pounded in a pestle (background) to release the grains. The resulting meal (foreground) is then sifted before being made into porridge and flatbreads.

(1889–1956) imposed foreign forms of government and attracted Christian missionaries to the region. Since 1983, when the latest round of Sudan's ongoing civil war erupted, the daily life of the Dinka has been severely disrupted by conflict.

Prewar Dinka daily life was based around the seasonal cycles of flooding on the Upper Nile. Each year the Dinka would move between permanent high-ground homesteads and temporary cattle camps. At the homesteads sorghum and corn were grown and the cattle kept in a corral at night. Fishing was also undertaken at these homesteads, supplementing the Dinka diet. In the dry season the younger male family members dispersed to widespread temporary cattle camps, while the elder community members remained in the permanent villages.

The Dinka are divided into several territorial groupings. Cutting across these territorial groups are kin groups, called clans, each of which recognizes either real or

DINKA CATTLE

As well as being of enormous economic importance, cattle are a central feature of Dinka social life. Transactions involving cattle—such as payments to secure a bride (bridewealth), sacrifices, and compensation payments—create and confirm Dinka social relations. The Dinka take great care of their cattle, cleaning them, decorating them with tassels and bells, and praising them in song. Of particular importance are oxen, whose horns are often made to grow into special shapes. On initiation into adulthood, each Dinka man is given an ox and takes the name of the ox's color pattern. The Dinka have a huge vocabulary for cattle color patterns, and they take great pride in finding elaborate new ways to describe such patterns. So, a Dinka man will not be content to be called simply by the basic name for his black ox ("ma car"), but will think up many other names to emphasize blackness. For example, he may be known as "thicket of the buffalo," suggesting the deep darkness of the forest in which the black buffalo resides.

A traditional Dinka ox song runs:

O Creator
Creator who created me in my mother's womb
Do not confront me with a bad thing
Show me the place of cattle,
So that I may grow my crops
And keep my herd.

Women construct a thatched home from savanna grass at a temporary cattle camp during the dry season.

Cattle are central to the way of life of both the Dinka and their neighbors the Nuer. Young men of these two peoples have traditionally undertaken cattle raids as part of their initiation rite. But with the tensions of Sudan's civil war and the spread of automatic weapons, these raids became more deadly.

mythical descent from a common ancestor. Clans may be represented in a number of territorial groupings and can further be divided into smaller descent lineages, often named for their founding mothers. Dinka clans fall into two categories—the priestly clans, and the commoner or warrior clans. The priestly clans are the sources of Dinka high priests, whose symbol is the fishing spear. These "masters of the fishing spear" are thought to have unusual powers and act as influential ritual leaders of the people.

CULTURE AND RELIGION

The Dinka recognize *jok* (spirits) of various kinds. The most important of these is Nhialic, meaning "sky" or "above," though Nhialic is also referred to as Aciek ("creator") or Wa ("father"). The Dinka also believe in a range of powers that are collectively known as *yeeth*. These *yeeth* include "clan divinities" (spirits directly related to each clan) and "free divinities" (spirits that may form relationships with individuals or families). The Dinka sacrifice livestock and pray to these divinities at various important life-cycle occasions, as well as at times of misfortune. Spirits may also possess individuals, sometimes resulting in that person becoming a prophet believed to have supernatural powers.

Since the 1920s the Dinka have been heavily exposed to Christian missionary activity and a significant missionary-educated class has emerged. These educated Dinka are often referred to as the "children of the missionaries" and have embraced a more Westernized culture. Yet despite the missionary influence, it is clear that the Dinka still hold on to many of their preexisting beliefs. Indeed, many Dinka probably accepted Christianity as much for the practical, material benefits of education and medicine as for its own sake. Moreover, becoming nominally Christian in Sudan is one way of resisting Islamic dominance.

SEE ALSO: Arabs; Baggara; Nuer; Oral literature.

MAJOR ISLAMIC FESTIVALS AND HOLY DAYS

Festival/Holy Day	Day/Month	Description
Al-Hijra	1 Muharram	A festival that commemorates the Hijra, the flight of the prophet Muhammad's ministry from Mecca to Medina.
Ashura	10 Muharram	A day of fasting for Sunni Muslims The Shia minority commemorate the martyrdom of Hussein, one of Muhammad's grandsons, on this day.
Lailat al-Miraj	27 Rajab	A festival that commemorates the Prophet's miraculous "Night Journey" from Mecca to Jerusalem, during which he ascended to heaven.
Lailat-ul-Barah	15 Shaban	The Night of Forgiveness involving prayer and the seeking of absolution of sins.
Lailat al-Qadr	27 Ramadan	A festival commemorating the night in which the Quran was revealed to the Prophet by the Angel Jibril (Gabriel).
Eid-ul-Fitr	1 Shawwal	A major festival that celebrates the end of Ramadan, the month of fasting between sunrise and sunset.
Eid-ul-Adha	10 Dhu al-Hijjah	A major festival that celebrates the hajj, the pilgrimage to Mecca.

The dates given are in the Islamic calendar, which operates on a 12-month lunar cycle rather than on the longer 365 day solar cycle found in the Western (Gregorian) calendar. Dates in the Islamic calendar therefore correspond to a different date in the Western calendar in any given year.

NORTH AFRICA BOASTS A HUGE NUMBER OF CEREMONIES, BOTH RELIGIOUS AND SECULAR. THESE RANGE FROM MAJOR PUBLIC FESTIVALS CELEBRATED ON PUBLIC HOLIDAYS, TO LOCAL, SMALL-SCALE EVENTS MARKING KEY STAGES IN PEOPLE'S LIVES.

HOLY DAYS AND FESTIVALS

Most of the population of North Africa are Sunni Muslims. Accordingly. the principal ceremonies and festivals of Islam are strictly observed and most people attend their local mosques for Friday prayers. In addition to commemorating the key events in the Islamic faith, many local festivals celebrate the lives of Muslim religious leaders. They often involve the ritual slaughter of sheep, an animal associated with the prophet Abraham, who is an important figure in Islam. Parades also take place at these local festivals, with people dressed as warriors

Coptic monks celebrate Christmas in the Egyptian monastery of St. Bishoi at Wadi el-Natrun. Copts believe that the Holy Family rested here while fleeing to Egypt to escape persecution by King Herod.

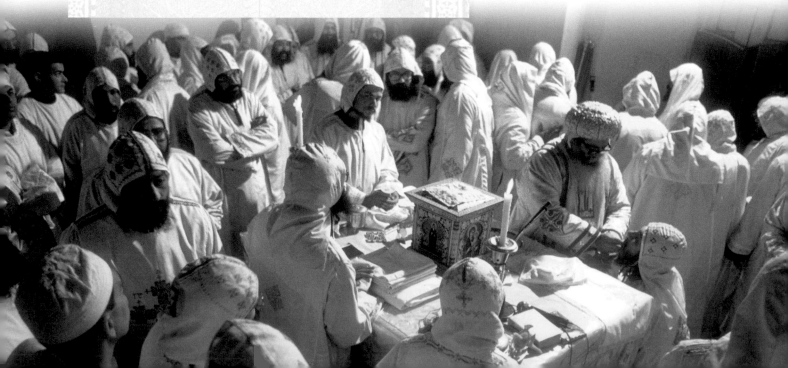

recalling the campaigns of conquest that brought Islam to North Africa from the mid-seventh century. Moroccan festivals known as *moussems* may take the form of religious gatherings and include prayer sessions. Yet other *moussems*, such as the camel markets, have a more commercial flavor.

The Coptic Church in Egypt has its own particular holy days and festivals, as well as observing the principal Christian feast days, such as Ascension, Christmas, Easter, Epiphany, and Pentecost. The Coptic Church uses its own calendar, which dates from the so-called "Era of Martyrs," a period from 284 C.E. onward when the Roman emperor Diocletian persecuted the Copts. As a result, the dates of the major Christian feast days are different, with Christmas, say, falling on January 7.

RITE-OF-PASSAGE CEREMONIES AND SEASONAL CELEBRATIONS

There is an enormous range of ceremonies marking various important stages in a person's life. These ceremonies are often called rites of passage and are associated with key events such as birth, initiation into adulthood, marriage, and death. At birth, Coptic Christians are baptized with water and confirmed as members of the Church. In Muslim weddings in Egypt the bride and groom are seated face to face, while a reader of the Quran ties their hands together with a handkerchief and prays that the marriage will be blessed. Among cattle herding societies such as the Nuer of Sudan, major celebrations of this kind are accompanied by the sacrifice of oxen. This occurs, for instance, during male initiation rites, where young men are admitted into the world of adults and once used to receive the horizontal forehead scars typical of Nuer men.

Seasonal rites that mark the annual cycle of nature are often linked to important events in the farming calendar such as harvest or planting. Often the purpose is to

THE IMILCHIL BRIDE FAIR

Every year, the Aït Hadiddou Berbers of the High Atlas mountains hold a special *moussem* at the town of Imilchil in Morocco. The Bride Fair is designed for women to find a suitable husband. It is a festive occasion, with dancing carrying on late into the evening. Imilchil is associated with a Muslim saint, Sidi Mohammed el-Merheni, who is believed to have had the ability to bless marriages and ensure their success, so during the fair prayers are offered outside the shrine dedicated to him. Widows and divorcees, who form the majority of the women and are distinguished by pointed hoods, are able to take a husband that evening if they can find a man they like. Virgins, however, must undergo a long process of courtship lasting a year before they can marry. Widows and divorcees are very much in demand, since the prospective husband is not required to pay any bridewealth to the bride's family when she remarries.

A veiled Berber bride-to-be at the Imilchil Bride Fair. Women are not "bought" at this festival; rather, marriage depends on mutual consent and family approval of the match.

give thanks for prosperity and ensure good conditions in the future. The *kujur* are important ritual specialists among the Nuba who are responsible for conducting rainmaking ceremonies to ensure that crops are well-watered.

MODERN FESTIVALS AND EVENTS

North Africa has a growing number of nonreligious festivals. Examples include film and music events such as the Cairo Film Festival in Egypt or the Festival of Sacred Music, held in Fez, Morocco. Marathon runs are gaining in popularity in Egypt, following the success of the annual Egyptian Marathon, held in February, and the Pharaonic Race, which is inspired by a seventh-century B.C.E. Egyptian hieroglyphic account of such a race that took place in ancient times. Other festivals have also been established to celebrate the ancient civilizations of the Nile, such as the Abu Simbel Festival, held twice annually on the site of a major Nubian temple complex built by the Pharaoh Ramses II.

SEE ALSO: Copts; Dance and song; Islam; Movies.

MAJOR WORKS AND THEIR AUTHORS

Title	Date	Author	Country
L'Etranger (The Foreigner)	1942	Albert Camus	Algeria
La Peste (The Plague)	1947		
Le Chapelet d'Ambre (The Amber Prayer Beads)	1949	Ahmed Sefrioui	Morocco
Le Fils du Pauvre (The Poor Man's Son)	1950	Mouloud Feraoun	Algeria
La Grande Maison (The Great House)	1952	Mohammed Dib	Algeria
Le Passé Simple (The Simple Past)	1954	Driss Chraibi	Morocco
Nedjma	1956	Kateb Yacine	Algeria
La Soif (Thirst)	1957	Assia Djebar	Algeria
La Répudiation (Repudiation)	1969	Rachid Boudjedra	Algeria
Dérision et Vertige (Ridicule and Dizziness)	1972	Jean Senac	Algeria
Le Livre du Sang (Blood's Book)	1979	Abdelkebir Khatibi	Morocco
Le Fleuve Detourné (The Diverted River)	1982	Rachid Mimouni	Algeria
Gloire des Sables (Glory of the Sands)	1982	Mustapha Tlili	Tunisia
L'Enfant de Sable (The Sand Child)	1985	Tahar Ben Jelloun	Morocco
The World's Embrace: Selected Poems	2003	Abdellatif Laabi	Morocco

The Tunisian writer Mustapha Tlili (b.1937), who now lives in New York, has also been a distinguished U.N. official and academic. One of his chief concerns is the need for dialogue between Islam and the West.

WRITERS FROM NORTH AFRICAN COUNTRIES UNDER FRENCH CONTROL BEGAN TO USE THE LANGUAGE OF THEIR COLONIAL MASTERS TO CALL FOR CHANGE AND FREEDOM. RECENT WORKS IN FRENCH FROM THE MAGHREB EXPLORE THE QUESTION OF POSTCOLONIAL IDENTITY.

BEGINNINGS

The development of French-language (Francophone) literature in North Africa is closely associated with the history of Algeria, Tunisia, and Morocco under French colonial rule. Francophone literature in North Africa therefore began as the product of French settlers and their descendants, the most famous of whom was the philosopher and author Albert Camus. Works like *L'Etranger* and *La Peste* treated major themes of philosophical and political interest (*La Peste*, for example, symbolizes in part the Nazi occupation of France). However, they also revealed the author's great love and knowledge of the landscape and climate of Algeria. Although Camus left the country after independence, other French writers like the poet Jean Senac remained, having supported the independence struggle.

THE FIRST MAGHREBI WRITERS

Although native Moroccan, Algerian, and Tunisian authors came from different linguistic and cultural backgrounds than French settler writers, many chose to write in French rather than their native Arabic or Berber. The colonial language allowed them to reach a much wider audience. Among the first indigenous writers in French was Ahmed Sefrioui, a Moroccan Berber. Sefrioui's short stories and longer works drew heavily on

BEUR LITERATURE

More than 6 million Muslims of North African descent now live in France and other western European countries. These include such famous authors as Tahar Ben Jalloun, Driss Chraibi, Mohammed Dib, and Abdellatif Laabi. "Beur literature" (*Beur* is French slang for "Arab") refers to the writings of the second- and third-generation descendants of these immigrants, especially those living in squalid, racially segregated suburban areas of Paris. Many novels of this movement draw on autobiographical experiences, and focus on the difficulties experienced by the Beurs in squaring their French, North African, and Muslim identities and heritages. Examples include Farida Belghoul's *Georgette!* (1986) and Paul Smaïl's *Vivre Me Tue* (Living Kills Me, 1997).

Morocco's rich storytelling tradition but did not contain any obvious political comment. As the hopes of the North African people for self-determination grew after World War II (1939–45), other writers looked at the impact of colonialism and cultural fusion in greater depth. These writers included Mohammed Dib, who was educated in the French school system of colonial Algeria before emigrating to France. His novels, such as *La Grande Maison* and *Qui Se Souvient de la Mer* (1962) address issues of human rights and justice under colonial rule. From the same era, Mouoloud Feraoun's *Le Fils du Pauvre* is still widely read in Algerian schools.

DECOLONIZATION AND POLITICAL PROTEST

The bloody Algerian War of Independence (1954–62) became a major theme of novels and poetry, but the period around decolonization was dominated by Kateb Yacine's *Nedjma*. Named for its leading female character, this novel examines the violence of Algerian society under colonial rule. A new, energetic group of writers later emerged who were associated with the student uprisings of 1968 in France. Among this group were Abdellatif Laabi, who later spent eight years in jail as a political prisoner in Morocco, and Rachid Boudjedra, author of the politically and socially critical *La Répudiation*. Together, this new wave of writers and the more established authors

A scene from the play La Femme Sauvage (1963) by the Algerian writer Kateb Yacine (1929–89). Yacine was a politically engaged writer, and his early plays were banned by the colonial authorities.

ensured that French-language literature in North Africa remained vibrant after the end of colonial rule. The 1970s and 1980s saw new writers come to prominence, such as Abdelkebir Khatibi, Tahar Ben Jelloun, Rachid Mimouni, Mustapha Tlili, and the region's leading female author, Assia Djebar.

WRITERS AND ISLAMIC EXTREMISM

Recent major themes in Algerian literature are the collapse of the one-party state and the civil war that erupted after the military coup of 1992 that was staged to keep Islamic fundamentalists from taking power. Some 60,000 people have died in this conflict; terrorists of the GIA (Groupe Islamique Armée, or Armed Islamic Group) also targeted intellectuals, causing a major impact on the literary scene. Recent works by Assia Djebar, Rachid Boudjedra, and Rachid Mimouni have all examined this crisis and criticized the rise of religious extremism.

SEE ALSO: Arabic literature; Movies; Oral literature.

FUR

FACT FILE

Population	It is thought that the Fur may number close to 1 million, many of whom now reside in refugee camps both within the Sudan and in neighboring Chad.
Religion	Islam
Language	Fur is only distantly related to other southern Sudanese Nilo-Saharan languages and many Fur now also speak local dialects of Arabic.

TIMELINE

c.1300	Arab invasions of the Sudan lead to establishment of Arab nomadic groups in the Darfur region.
c.1600	Establishment of Darfur Sultanate.
1750	Darfur expands to the north and south.
1821	Turkish invasion of Sudan by Mohammed Ali.
1874	Egypt annexes Darfur.
1881–85	Mahdist revolution in the Sudan.
1889	British establish Anglo-Egyptian government in Sudan.
1916	Anglo-Egyptian government annexes Darfur sultanate.
1956	Sudan wins independence from Britain.
1962–72	First Sudanese civil war.
1983	Islamic law (Sharia) imposed by Khartoum government, sparking the Second Sudanese civil war.
2003	Prospect of peace in southern Sudan provokes unrest in other regions, particularly Darfur, as anti-government forces clash with the Janjaweed, the government-backed militias. Civilians bear the brunt of the conflict.
2005	As the Second Sudanese civil war ends in the south, civil war continues in Darfur, with an estimated 2 million displaced and 180,000 dead.

THE FUR INHABIT THE AREA AROUND THE JEBEL MARRA AND JEBEL SI MOUNTAINS IN WESTERN SUDAN'S DARFUR REGION (MEANING "LAND OF THE FUR"). SINCE 2003, DARFUR HAS BEEN RAVAGED BY INTENSE INTERETHNIC CONFLICT AND MANY FUR HAVE BEEN DISPLACED.

HISTORY

Little is known about the origins of the Fur, although they are thought to be an African people who, over time, became intermixed with various Arab groups that moved into the area from the 14th century on. The language of the Fur is only remotely related to other southern Sudanese languages and has likely been greatly modified through contact with other African and Arabic speaking peoples. Before colonial rule (1916) the Fur were ruled by a sultan (Muslim king) who at times also ruled over neighboring groups. More recently Fur chiefs have been incorporated into the central administrative system of Darfur. Since 2003 Darfur has been ravaged by a bloody civil war, sparked by tension between settled farmers and nomadic herders. The war has displaced more than 2 million people, many of them Fur.

SOCIETY AND DAILY LIFE

The Fur are settled farmers who grow millet on the slopes of the Jebel Marra and in the surrounding area. The region is very arid, so crop growing is often aided by the construction of small terraces (to prevent water run-off) and irrigation canals. Land

Fur women displaced by the civil war in Darfur collect firewood near Nyala. The Darfur conflict was not caused primarily by ethnic tensions, but by a clash between sedentary farmers and nomadic cattle herders over precious land.

is administered by the local chief and all adult members of society (men and women) have access to land. Husbands and wives generally cultivate their own land individually and each wife grows crops to support her own children. Women often brew millet beer, which is either exchanged for money or used to hold a beer-party during which people from outside the village come to help with farm labor.

CULTURE AND RELIGION

The Fur are Muslims; they adopted Islam after being conquered by the Kanem-Borno empire in the mid-13th century. Accordingly, they have long had Islamic forms of government, with a political hierarchy of sheikhs (chiefs) who were, in the past, subordinate to the Fur sultan. The fact that the Fur were Muslim enabled them to interact on an equal footing with the surrounding nomadic peoples who spoke Arabic and claimed a

FUR OR BAGGARA?

Before war broke out in Darfur in 2003, the Fur enjoyed good economic relations with their nomadic, cattle-herding neighbors, the Baggara. The Fur often invest any profits from surplus crop production in cattle. However, because Fur territory is not suited to cattle herding, the Fur came to a mutually beneficial arrangement with the Baggara. The Fur loaned their cattle to the Baggara, who herded them with their own in return for the milk the animals produced. Interestingly, in the past, once the herd of a Fur farmer reached a certain size it made economic sense for the Fur to give up his status as a settled farmer and adopt a nomadic way of life. Yet in doing so the Fur ceased to be Fur and became a Baggara. This ethnic fluidity has likely occurred for centuries and is testament to the fundamental unity of the two populations, despite their cultural and economic differences.

more direct Arab descent. There is no physical difference between the Fur and the nomads; however, the Arab/non-Arab ethnic division has been exploited during the Darfur conflict in Darfur, leading to Muslims fighting their fellow Muslims.

SEE ALSO: Arabs; Baggara; Dinka.

TIMELINE

622 The prophet Muhammad sets up a community in Medina; this hijra or "withdrawal" marks the beginning of the Islamic calendar.

661–751 The Umayyad caliphate, based in Damascus, controls an area stretching from Spain to the west to India to the east, including all of North Africa. Kairouan (Tunisia) is founded as a local administrative center.

711 Arabs secure control over all of North Africa.

751–61 The Abbasids overthrow the Umayyads and set up their capital at Baghdad in 761, shifting the focus of the empire away from the Mediterranean.

800–909 Although nominally ruling as an Abbasid governor, al-Aghlab sets up a quasi-independent dynasty, the Aghlabids, in Kairouan, which reaches a height of prosperity and culture. A House of Wisdom is established for the study of medicine, engineering, translation and astronomy.

909–1171 The Fatimid dynasty (named for the daughter of the prophet Muhammad) takes control of North Africa, based first in modern Tunisia then in modern Cairo. They dispatch groups such as the Banu Hillal to spread their (Shi'ite) form of Islam, strengthening Arab culture and Islam throughout northern Africa.

11th century The Almoravids, a Berber dynasty from Mauretania, conquer the western half of North Africa and Spain, and spread Islam south of the Sahara.

1140s–1250 The Almohads, a Berber dynasty from the Atlas mountains, defeat the Almoravids. They conquer all of northern Africa as well as Spain.

1881–85 Religious leader al-Mahdi conducts a major holy war against British and Egyptian rule in Sudan.

1960s–present Violent sporadic clashes between governments of North African states and Islamist extremists.

ISLAM WAS BROUGHT TO NORTH AFRICA BY ARAB ARMIES IN THE SEVENTH AND EIGHTH CENTURIES. WITHIN FOUR CENTURIES OF THEIR CONQUEST, MOST OF THE REGION'S INHABITANTS WERE MUSLIM. RECENT YEARS HAVE SEEN CONFLICTS ERUPT BETWEEN SUPPORTERS OF A RADICAL FORM OF ISLAM AND THEIR SECULAR (NONRELIGIOUS) GOVERNMENTS.

The faith of Islam (meaning "submission to the will of God") was founded by the Prophet Muhammad (c.570–632) in the Arabian peninsula in 622 C.E. Spreading rapidly from its original heartland, within 500 years Islam had expanded to cover an area stretching from Senegal in the west to the eastern borders of Persia. North Africa was one of the first areas to be conquered by the caliphs—the religious–political leaders who succeeded Muhammad—as the Arabs greatly extended the area under their control.

HISTORY

Before the arrival of Islam, North Africa was a patchwork of different religions. Most people in the coastal cities such as Carthage, Cyrene, and Alexandria, which had once been part of the Roman Empire, were Christian. These cities also had sizable Jewish populations. In addition, Berber groups of the interior followed preexisting religions. Arab armies rapidly spread Islam across North Africa, which was conquered by 711. The strongest resistance to the Arab

One of the Five Pillars of Islam—the duties every Muslim must perform—is prayer (Arabic: Salah). Prayer is conducted five times daily; if a Muslim cannot attend a mosque, he or she may offer individual prayers, facing the holy city of Mecca in Arabia. Here, a Bedouin prays in the Sinai desert.

The Sultan Hassan mosque and madrasah in Cairo, with its many minarets (towers). Minarets were added to mosques so that officials known as muezzin could call the faithful to prayer.

invasion was in the west among the Berbers, many of whom were displaced from the coast into the mountains and desert.

Although many people in North Africa quickly converted to Islam, Christians and Jews were not forced to renounce their religion. Islam regards followers of these religions as "People of the Book," who also believe in the one creator deity (Allah/God/ Jehovah), and many prophets such as Abraham and Moses are recognized by all three faiths. Accordingly, they were allowed to continue practicing their faith but a

CAIRO—A CENTER OF ISLAMIC SCHOLARSHIP

Islam was brought to Egypt by the Arab armies that overran North Africa from around 640 onward. These forces founded the military garrison town of al-Fustat, which became the seed of the modern metropolis of Cairo—now the largest city in Africa. A key development in the city's religious life took place in 1171, when the famous Arab commander Saladin took Egypt from the Fatimids—a dissident Shi'ite Islamic sect from Tunisia who had ruled the region for 200 years—and reestablished orthodox Sunni Islam. This change was reinforced by the founding of many madrasahs, colleges for the teaching of Islam, which were often attached to mosques. Cairo's growing reputation as a major center of Islamic learning was reinforced during the Mamluke period (1250–1517), when scholars from both the West (driven out by the Christian reconquest of Moorish Spain) and from the East (fleeing Baghdad and Damascus as Mongol armies advanced) took refuge there. Today, the city has more than 500 mosques; one of the most renowned is the Sultan Hassan mosque and madrasah, built in 1356–63.

jizya (poll tax) was levied on them as non-Muslims. Therefore, Arab expansion into North Africa was not a war of conversion but rather one of conquest, aiming to place an Islamic social and political framework on the region.

Egypt was under Muslim control by 642, just 10 years after the death of Muhammad. This rapid change was due in large part to tension between the rulers of the country, who were Orthodox Christians, and the majority of the populace, who were Coptic Christians (see COPTS). The people welcomed the Arab conquerors as liberators, and in many cases converted to their faith. Later, the dynamic Umayyad dynasty, founded in Damascus in Syria by the fifth caliph Muawiyah (602–80), spread Arab rule farther westward along the North African coast. In 670 an Arab army founded the city of Kairouan, south of modern Tunis, both as a military stronghold and as a political and cultural center (see ARCHITECTURE).

Under the Umayyad caliphate, Arabs in North Africa formed a ruling elite that enjoyed financial and political power over the original native peoples, such as the Berbers. As a result, new converts felt alienated and soon demanded their rights as members of a religion that is based on the equality of all believers. When the Umayyads were overthrown by the Abbasid dynasty in 750, Arabs lost their privileged status. However, by this time Arabic had become firmly established throughout North Africa as the language of science, literature, and government.

However, the Abbasids found it increasingly difficult to maintain control over the far-flung Muslim lands, especially in North Africa. The Idrisid emirs in the northwest (an area known as the Maghreb) broke away in 789 to found their own caliphate, which adhered to the rival Shi'ite branch of Islam. The governor of Kairouan, though nominally under Abbasid leadership,

ruled virtually independently for decades before the Aghlabid emirs of the region finally declared full independence in 800. In Egypt the Tulunid and later the Fatimid dynasty also asserted their independence from their Abbasid masters. At the same time, many Berber converts adopted the Kharijite form of Islam in protest against heavy taxation and alienation. This radical movement, which rejected the authority of the caliph, allowed them to resist Arab political domination.

MARRIAGE AND FAMILY

The core of Islam is formed by five fundamental duties that all believers must perform, commonly known as the Five Pillars of Islam: the expression of faith, daily prayer at five appointed times, fasting during Ramadan (see below), giving to charity, and pilgrimage to the holy city of Mecca (in modern Saudi Arabia).

Concepts of family life are based on the Quran and the prophet Muhammad's life. The family unit consists of a man, his wife or wives (up to four are allowed), and their children—but the benefits of family life are seen as extending not just to blood relations but also to the world-wide family of Muslims (ummah).

FESTIVALS AND CEREMONIES

Muslim celebration days are fixed by a lunar calendar, meaning that the date on which they fall varies according to the moon. A major festival is Ramadan, a month during which neither food nor water is taken from sunrise to sunset. Because fasting, and in particular not drinking any water, is very demanding in hot weather, people often radically alter their schedules, sleeping through the hottest hours of the day and working during the cooler periods. The festival that marks the end of the month of fasting—Eid ul-Fitr—is a major celebration. In general it is looked upon as a day for the

In the Egyptian capital Cairo, thousands of Muslims gather to pray in the open air at dawn on the first day of the Eid ul-Fitr festival. This four-day celebration marks the end of the holy month of Ramadan, and is observed by Muslims worldwide.

family, starting with special prayers at the mosque, followed by a festive lunch at the house of the senior member of the family. In Egypt, where celebrations extend over four days, special biscuits are made to give to friends and relatives, and while the men go to the mosque the women prepare the fish that forms the centerpiece of the festive lunch.

Another important festival on the Islamic calendar, Eid ul-Adha or Eid ul-Kebir, commemorates the sacrifice that the prophet Abraham was prepared to make when God asked him to kill his son Isaac, before God intervened at the last moment and offered a sheep for sacrifice instead. Each family head kills a sheep and donates some of its meat to the poor; typically the sheep is roasted or, in Morocco, made into a stew (tagine) in a ceramic dish with a tall conical lid, using raisins, almonds, honey, and spices.

SEE ALSO: *Arabic literature; Arabs; Architecture; Berbers; Calligraphy; Christianity; Copts; Festival and ceremony; Jews; Marriage and the family.*

NORTH AFRICAN ISLAMIC EXTREMISTS

Since the first independent states were founded in North Africa following the end of the colonial era, there have been violent tensions between supporters of Arab nationalism, who believe in the ideal of secular (nonreligious) government and radical Islamists, who wish to establish states based on Sharia (Islamic law). The Muslim Brotherhood was founded in 1928 in Egypt to promote the goal of the religious state. One of its members, Sayyid Qutb (1906–66) was imprisoned by the Arab nationalist government of Gamal Abdel Nasser; following his release, Qutb continued to develop his radical thought, which has had a strong influence on modern Egyptian terrorist organizations such as Takfir wal Hijra, Gamaa al-Islamiya, and Egyptian Islamic Jihad. Such groups have attempted to assassinate Egyptian leaders and attacked Western tourists. In Algeria, a similar struggle has been waged by the GIA (Groupe Islamique Armée, or Armed Islamic Group) against the government after the 1991 elections were annulled when it seemed the Islamic Salvation Front party was heading for victory. These violent extremists, who have very little popular support, regard anyone but themselves as kaffir (non-believers) who should be executed for their blasphemy, and so have massacred even their fellow citizens. They are linked to al-Qaeda through Osama bin Laden's second-in-command, the Egyptian physician Ayman al-Zawahiri (b.1951), who was formerly head of Egyptian Islamic Jihad.

JEWISH POPULATION BY COUNTRY

Algeria	fewer than 100
Egypt	100
Ethiopia	100
Morocco	5,600
Tunisia	1,500
Rest of region	fewer than 100

NORTH AFRICA WAS ONCE HOME TO A JEWISH POPULATION OF 600,000–700,000. YET AFTER THE NATIONS OF NORTH AFRICA WON THEIR INDEPENDENCE, MANY JEWS EMIGRATED TO THE NEW STATE OF ISRAEL OR TO FRANCE. TODAY, LESS THAN 10,000 JEWISH PEOPLE REMAIN.

The Tunisian island of Djerba is home to a large part of the country's remaining Jewish population. The el-Ghriba synagogue there has long been a focus for the community; in 2002, a group linked to al-Qaeda bombed it, killing 17 people.

THE CAIRO GENIZAH ARCHIVE

Jewish religious law forbids the destruction of texts mentioning God. Instead, they must be placed in a special storeroom in the synagogue before eventual burial in a cemetery. One such ancient depository (Genizah, "hiding-place" in Hebrew) in the Ezra Synagogue in the Cairo suburb of Fostat contained some 250,000 medieval documents, which were preserved by the dry Egyptian climate. Rediscovered in 1896, these texts offer a rare insight into the community life and intercontinental trading links of Cairo's Jewish community from the 11th to 13th centuries. They are a priceless resource for historians, and study of the manuscripts continues to this day.

EARLY HISTORY

North Africa has been home to Jewish people for more than 2,500 years. Egypt played a prominent part in the history of the people of Israel, as recounted in the Hebrew Bible; archaeological evidence shows that Jewish mercenaries serving near modern Aswan worshipped at a local version of the Temple of Jerusalem in the seventh century B.C.E. By Roman times, Alexandria in Egypt was home to a substantial Jewish population, including the translators of the Hebrew Bible into Greek and the philosopher Philo. The relations of the Jews with their Greek and Egyptian neighbors, and with their Roman rulers, were often difficult (notably during the Jewish revolts in Judea in 66–73 and 132–135 C.E.), but the Jews were also accorded many privileges. Inscriptions and papyri confirm that both Egypt and northeastern Libya (Cyrenaica) had a large Jewish presence and that this extended to major Roman cities in the Maghreb such as Carthage. There, some local Berber communities also converted to Judaism during the first millennium C.E., while in Ethiopia the Falasha people are thought to have converted from Christianity around the 14th to 16th centuries.

JEWS UNDER MUSLIM RULE

Like Christians, Jews were offered protection by the Muslim Arabs after they overran North Africa in the seventh and eighth centuries. Jews were regarded as "people of the Book" (namely, fellow believers in One God) and so were allowed to practice their religion in return for payment of a poll-tax known as the jizya. Across the region Jews were heavily involved in trade, banking, and in making jewelry and clothing, areas in which they were still active well into the 20th century. Some individuals occupied prominent positions, for example as government ministers and physicians, including the famous Jewish scholar, Moses

Maimonides (1135–1204). In northwest Africa, however, Jews were increasingly confined to closed areas of towns called mellahs, in part for their own safety during periodic anti-Semitic rioting, but also because this made it easier for local rulers to tax and control them. Restrictions were also placed on travel, dress, and riding horses or donkeys, and were only revoked in the colonial period. Another key event in Jewish history in the Maghreb was the sudden influx of refugees following the expulsion of all Jews from Spain by King Ferdinand and Queen Isabella in 1492. These new incomers swelled the existing population of Mizrahim (Jews who had always lived in the Middle East and North Africa). The Jews of Spanish and Portuguese descent (including the family of Maimonides, who settled in Morocco) were known as Sephardim; the Sephardic community around Chaouen in Morocco continued to speak medieval Spanish into the 1920s.

THE 19TH AND 20TH CENTURIES

The advent of European colonial rule brought new Jewish settlers to North Africa, especially to Egypt, where merchants and professionals settled in Alexandria and Cairo. Yet the seizure of private enterprises by the Egyptian nationalist regime of Gamal Abdel Nasser, which took power in 1954, plus recurring armed conflict between Egypt and the newly founded state of Israel (1948, 1956) caused many Jews to leave Egypt. Most of the well-established Jewish community throughout North Africa soon followed suit, especially after the Six-Day War of 1967 between Israel and its Arab neighbors. By then only some 3 percent of Egypt's former population of 75,000 Jews remained. Today only tiny Jewish communities still exist in North Africa, with few viable synagogues.

See also: Arabs; Islam.

LEATHER HAS BEEN USED BY CRAFTSPEOPLE IN NORTH AFRICA FOR AT LEAST 7,000 YEARS. IN MEDIEVAL TIMES, THE REGION BECAME KNOWN FOR THE SOFT "MOROCCO" LEATHER (IMPORTED FROM WEST AFRICA) THAT WAS MADE INTO BAGS AND BOOK BINDINGS. NORTH AFRICAN LEATHERWORKERS NOW SUPPLY A THRIVING TOURIST MARKET WITH MANY DIFFERENT GOODS.

HISTORY

Leather is not as resilient as other, more durable materials, such as stone and metal; consequently, very few early examples of leatherwork have survived. Even so, some archaeological sites and historical sources give an impression of how leather was used by ancient peoples in North Africa.

For example, sandals and other leather items have been found at archeological excavations of ancient Egyptian sites, while

Roman historical accounts reveal that the Berbers used white leather shields in combat. Vegetable tanning, a process still used in parts of North Africa today was invented in Egypt around 400 B.C.E. The technique reached its height in medieval Morocco and Muslim Spain, although it has been partially replaced by chemical tanning since the 19th century. The spread of Islam into Africa introduced new forms of leather crafts, such as bookbinding (paper, which was invented in China, was also an Islamic introduction). Many fine examples of such work can be seen in manuscripts preserved in North African museums. Some of these date to before the 11th century.

Form the mid-16th century on, the region of the North African coast known as Tripoli (in present-day Libya) exported "Morocco" leather, which actually came from the cities of the Hausa in West Africa, to the Ottoman empire and Europe.

LEATHERWORK TODAY

North Africa is one of the world's major regions for the production of leather goods, for export, for local use and for tourists as souvenirs. Cities such as Marrakech and Fez in Morocco are among the most renowned manufacturing centers. The first stage of production takes place at the tanneries, or *chouaras*, where the animal hides are cleaned and treated. This process often takes place away from the residential quarters of the town because of the very unpleasant, pungent smell that it creates. Craftsmen then use the material to fashion a wide range of

Traditional slippers known as babouches *(left) are made throughout North Africa from soft leather, and are very popular items for the tourist market. Their uppers are often decorated with sequins.*

These dye pits (right) at a tannery in the medina— the old heart of the city—in Fez in Morocco have remained unchanged for centuries. Animal hides that have been tanned (treated with chemicals to make leather) are dipped in natural vegetable dyes.

WAFAA EL-HOUDAYBI

The Moroccan artist Wafaa El-Houdaybi is known for using leather in her art, and has exhibited in galleries in London and elsewhere. Her work, involving painted leather and canvas disks and henna, explores the culture and history of North Africa, and in particular makes extensive use of Berber symbols. Her pieces combine indigenous, Islamic, and contemporary artistic styles. According to the artist, her work celebrates the natural forces within the material, which are awakened when the observer looks at the art object.

goods including traditional slippers, bags, and upholstery for desks and other pieces of furniture.

Elaborately decorated leatherwork is strongly associated with equestrian activities. Foremost among these are *fantasias*—festivals held throughout North Africa that are renowned for their impressive displays of horsemanship. Participants wear tall, embroidered leather boots, often in bright colors, and sit on elaborately decorated leather saddles. Tunisia in particular was once well known for its production of highly ornate saddles. However, this craft has largely died out in more recent times.

In common with the rest of the Islamic world, in North Africa copies of the Quran are frequently bound in sheepskin covers decorated with gold leaf designs. Islam regards not only the text of the Quran as sacred but also the physical object of the Quran. Accordingly, it must be treated with great respect. The thick leather bindings, which usually have flaps that fold over to protect the front edges of the book, ensure that the Quran is not marked or damaged. The gold tooling on the binding also stresses the specialness and sanctity of the scripture.

SEE ALSO: Arabs; Berbers; Festival and ceremony.

	Birth rate/ 1,000 population*	Infant mortality Deaths/1,000 births*	Fertility rate: Children born/woman (2005 est.)	HIV/AIDS in 2003 Living with (est.)	Deaths from HIV/ AIDS in 2003 (est.)
Algeria	17	31	1.9	9,100	under 500
Egypt	23	33	2.9	12,000	700
Libya	27	25	3.3	10,000	NA
Morocco	22	42	2.7	15,000	NA
Sudan	35	62	4.8	400,000	23,000
Tunisia	16	25	1.8	1,000	under 200

* per annum (2005 estimate)

I N NORTH AFRICA, THE DOMINANT SOCIAL INFLUENCE IS ISLAM, WHICH LAYS DOWN STRICT GUIDELINES REGARDING MARRIAGE AND THE FAMILY. RECENTLY TENSION HAS ARISEN BETWEEN A LIBERAL VIEW OF WOMEN AND THEIR ROLE AND TRADITIONAL ATTITUDES. IN ALGERIA AND EGYPT, THERE HAVE BEEN MAJOR CLASHES BETWEEN SOCIAL REFORMERS AND RELIGIOUS FUNDAMENTALISTS.

A Berber man, his wife, and their child cross the Moroccan desert to go to visit a doctor. Conditions in North Africa are harsh, and infant mortality remains high in some parts of the region.

SOCIAL STATUS AND THE FAMILY

As a general rule, North African societies are strongly based around the man as the head of the family. Islam teaches that the family is at the very center of society and must be placed before all other social institutions. It also confirms male authority, and states that inheritance should occur through the male (patrilineal) line of descent. A Muslim's family is often their principal source of prestige, honor, and sense of identity. Non-Muslim societies in North Africa, chiefly in southern Sudan, also take this approach, although the women's status is usually higher than among Muslim groups. Berbers, although Muslims, differ from the Arab majority in that some follow matrilineal rules of inheritance; for example Berber women usually have more authority than their Arab counterparts.

The concept of *haram*, meaning "sacred" or "forbidden," and the related idea of *harim*, the area of the house where women are secluded from public gaze, play an important role in Muslim societies in North Africa. Male family members see it as their duty to protect the honor of their female relatives. Women often wear a veil (dressing modestly is called *hijab*) to prevent them from being seen by unrelated men. Among nomadic Bedouins, women travel in enclosed shelters on the backs of camels. This practice is not strictly observed by non-Arab Muslims, such as the Baggara of Sudan or the Berbers, whose women do not wear veils, travel openly and have few rules requiring them to wear modest dress.

MARRIAGE PRACTICES

Most North African peoples practice polygyny (the marriage of a man to more than one wife), and it is legal in all countries of the region except Tunisia. Although Islamic law allows a man to have up to four wives, as long as he is able to provide for and treat them all equally, polygyny is actually practiced by very few Muslims. Polygyny is also practiced by the non-Islamic societies of southern Sudan.

Bridewealth is a common custom throughout North Africa, being practiced in Muslim and non-Muslim societies alike. This is a payment made to the family of the women by her husband, and although sometimes thought of as "buying" a wife, it is perhaps better seen as a compensation to her kin for the loss of her labor. Among nomadic populations, such as the Nuer and the Baggara, cattle are the usual form of payment and the number of cattle a man owns usually dictates the number of wives he is able to take. In more settled populations money or valuable objects take the place of livestock. As a result of the need for bridewealth, polygyny is often confined to the wealthier members of society, whether they are Muslims or non-Muslims.

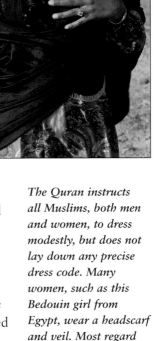

The Quran instructs all Muslims, both men and women, to dress modestly, but does not lay down any precise dress code. Many women, such as this Bedouin girl from Egypt, wear a headscarf and veil. Most regard hijab *as an expression of their faith and their devotion to Allah.*

SEE ALSO: *Berbers; Festival and ceremony; Islam; Nuer.*

NUER "GHOST MARRIAGE"

The Nuer, a Nilotic cattle-herding people from southern Sudan, follow a marriage custom known as "ghost marriage" (or leviratic marriage). According to this, if a man dies, his wife is free to marry another man, often her deceased husband's brother, and have children with him. However, the children are generally regarded as the offspring of the deceased husband rather than his replacement. Their family-tree relationships are reckoned as if they were descended from the deceased husband and they inherit any rights and property from him as well. The dead husband is referred to as the "social father." Since Nuer women do not in most cases have any wealth of their own, they will often marry a relative of their former spouse so that they can continue to hold property, theoretically in the name of their dead husbands.

THE PRODUCTION OF METAL OBJECTS IN NORTH AFRICA IS PART OF DIVERSE TRADITION THAT GOES BACK THOUSANDS OF YEARS. BRASS HAS LONG BEEN FAVORED TO MAKE EVERYDAY OBJECTS, SUCH AS PLATTERS, JUGS, AND BOWLS. TODAY A WIDE VARIETY OF ORNATE METAL ARTIFACTS ARE OFFERED FOR SALE TO TOURISTS IN THE MARKETS OF NORTH AFRICAN CITIES.

HISTORY

The earliest items were made from native metals such as gold, which have been found in prehistoric graves in Egypt that date to before 4000 B.C.E. Soon thereafter copper began to be smelted and used for a range of everyday utensils and vessels. The use of gold and silver was restricted to the ruling elite; these metals were also made into religious artifacts for temples. Bronze, which is much harder than copper, began to be adopted in Egypt after 2000 B.C.E. and spread into northeastern Libya and northern Sudan at the same time. Iron, which was being smelted from its ore in the Near East by 1400 B.C.E., only came into general use some centuries later, and was taken up in North Africa from around 700 B.C.E. It was introduced into the Maghreb by the Phoenicians, and Carthage became a major center of iron production.

From around 800 C.E. on, metalworking traditions in North Africa were heavily influenced by those of the Islamic world. Under Islam, representations of living things by artists were disapproved of. Accordingly, craftsmen who worked in metal concentrated on making elaborate and ornately decorated nonfigurative objects such as jewelry, vessels, and furniture, rather than representations of human or animal forms. Objects were often embossed with inscriptions in the Kufic script (see CALLIGRAPHY), for example a blessing on the patron who commissioned the work of art. Verses from the Quran were also common. Muslim craftsmen reached great levels of sophistication in applying decorative techniques such as inlay and engraving. The inlay technique involves embedding designs of soft metal (copper, gold, and especially silver) into the surface of objects made of harder metal such as brass or bronze. This was often achieved through the labor-intensive process of chiseling out grooves into which thin wires of the softer metal were then hammered. Inlay and engraving are still applied in contemporary North African metalwork.

Relatively few vessels and other objects from North Africa's past that were made of precious metals have survived, since Islam does not allow a person to be buried with material possessions. Rather, gold and silver objects were melted down and the metal used to make new artifacts.

Berber daggers (koummya) have characteristically curved blades double-edged blades. Their embossed and inlaid silver scabbards make them masterpieces of the metalworker's art.

RACHID KORAÏCHI

The Algerian sculptor Rachid Koraïchi (b.1947) is a North African artist who has won international acclaim. Koraïchi mainly uses metal as the medium for his work. *Steel Talismans*, one of his best-known pieces, takes its inspiration from the writing tablets that are commonly used to teach the Quran in Islamic schools (madrasahs) in North Africa. The calligraphy used in this work, however, is not in Arabic, but rather is a mixture of symbols and hieroglyphs of the artist's own invention. These express his sense of individuality, one of his favorite themes. Koraïchi now lives in exile in Paris, and his work has been shown in exhibitions throughout Europe.

METALWORK TODAY

The souks, or marketplaces, of North Africa's cities are well known for producing a wide variety of metal items, ranging from small copper jugs and teapots to enormous brass doors. Some manufacturing centers such as Meknès in Morocco have become famous worldwide.

Berber craftsmen are celebrated for their fine jewelry, particularly in silver. Its decoration often signifies membership of a regional group and items such as necklaces are worn on special occasions. The *hela*, a silver clasp worn by Berber women, is thought to bring the wearer beauty and fertility and protect her from the "evil eye" (a form of harmful envy that may be directed consciously or unconsciously by a living person). In the Sahara the long sabers made by the Berbers and Tuareg are popular with collectors. Today they are often produced from scrap steel reclaimed from vehicles abandoned in the desert. Everyday metal utensils are also popular, such as the *situle*, a copper vessel with a tall spout and handle that is used to carry water by the women of the Atlas mountains in Morocco.

The non-Muslim Nilotic peoples of southern Sudan have their own metalworking traditions. The Dinka and Nuer are known for their brass-wire jewelry, which is made from recycled telephone lines and cartridge cases. It is commonly fashioned into bracelets that are worn around arms and legs. This causes the limbs to swell slightly, a feature that is considered attractive in Nuer and Dinka society.

For many centuries, North African craftspeople have used copper and brass (an alloy of copper and zinc) to make jugs, bowls, candlesticks, and other utensils. Here, two boys wait for customers at a market stall in Cairo, Egypt, selling copper vessels and platters.

SEE ALSO: *Arabs; Berbers; Calligraphy; Dinka; Nuer; Textiles.*

MOVIES

NORTH AFRICAN MOVIES AND MOVIEMAKERS

Title	Date	Director	Country
Leila	1927	Stephan Rosti	Egypt
A Happy Day	1940	Mohammed Karim	Egypt
The Immortal Song	1959	Henry Baraket	Egypt
Dawn of the Damned	1965	Ahmed Rachedi	Algeria
Aziza	1977	Abdellatif Ben Amar	Tunisia
Leila and the Others	1978	Sid Ali Mazif	Algeria
Reed Dolls	1981	Jilali Ferhati	Morocco
The Beautiful Days of Sheherazade	1982	Mustapha Derkaoui	Morocco
Adieu Bonaparte	1985	Youssef Chahine	Egypt

MOVIEMAKING IN NORTH AFRICA BEGAN IN THE EARLY 20TH CENTURY. TODAY, FILMS REMAIN A POPULAR FORM OF ENTERTAINMENT ACROSS THE REGION AND HAVE ALSO BEEN USED TO VOICE SOCIAL CRITICISM.

HISTORY

Egyptian cinema has long dominated the North African movie world, making popular mainstream films from the early 20th century on. The first truly Egyptian film was Stephen Rosti's *Leila* (1927), a melodrama of love and betrayal that gave rise to a long line of similar movies. Egyptian cinema boomed when talking pictures began to be produced in the 1930s. Egyptian singers, already famous across the Arab world from radio shows, appeared on screen to popular acclaim. Great investment was made at this time in training, technology, and new studios.

Today Egypt remains at the forefront of Arab cinema. The annual Cairo International Film festival, inaugurated in 1976, is well attended. Egypt has also produced one of the leading Arab movie makers, Youssef Chahine, whose independent and challenging works include *Cairo Central Station* (1958), *Saladin* (1963), and *Adieu Bonaparte* (1985).

A poster outside a movie theater in the Egyptian capital Cairo. Egypt has by far the largest motion picture industry in North Africa. Although most of its output is comedy and light entertainment, important writers such as Naguib Mahfouz and Tawfiq al-Hakim have also written movie scripts.

EGYPT'S MOVIE STARS

Throughout the second half of the 20th century, the first lady of Egyptian cinema was Faten Hamama, who starred in films such as *A Happy Day* (1940), *The Immortal Song* (1959), *The Sin* (1964), *No Condolences For Women* (1979) and *The Night Of Fatma's Arrest* (1984). In 1953 she worked alongside a relatively unknown Syrian–Lebanese Christian called Michel Chalroub. Chalroub was later to marry Hamama and convert to Islam. On doing so he changed his name to Omar Sharif and went on to become one of the best-known products of Egyptian cinema, appearing in numerous Hollywood films. Together they starred in *The Black Waters* (1956), *Night Without Sleep* (1958) and *River Of Love* (1960).

NORTH AFRICAN CINEMA TODAY

Modern North African cinema is still affected by censorship, poor funding, and limited scope for release beyond the Arab world. Despite these problems, the second half of the 20th century saw the growth of a new, postcolonial Arab cinema. This new socially aware cinema aims to be a voice for the people, showing real lives and addressing critical social issues.

Moviemaking in Algeria was greatly stimulated by the docu-drama *The Battle of Algiers* (1965) by the Italian director Gillo Pontecorvo; based on the memoirs of an independence fighter and filmed in Algiers, this powerful movie had a major influence on home-grown cinema. Algerian state-run cinema thereafter produced movies on the history of colonialism and the struggle for independence. Such films include *Dawn Of The Damned* (1965) and *The Opium And The Baton* (1969) by Ahmed Rachedi; and *Wind From The Aurès* (1966) by Mohamed Lakhdar-Hamina. More recent Algerian films of interest include *Leila And The Others* (1978), which showed a new feminist perspective of women gaining freedom by working outside the home and *Touchia* (1993) by Rachid Benhadj, which criticized intolerance and repression against women.

Tunisia also has a state-sponsored cinema, and hosts the biennial Carthage Film Festival, which began in 1966. The country also has a thriving amateur film movement out of which have come films such as Ferid Boughedir's *Camera Arabe* (1987) and Nouri Bouzid's *Man Of Ashes* (1987), which deals with masculinity and child abuse and shows an era in Tunisia when Jews and Arabs coexisted peacefully.

Moroccan film makers have produced critically acclaimed movies such as Mohammed Reggab's *The Hairdresser From a Poor District* (1982); Taieb Sakkiki's *Zeft* (1984); Mustapha Derkaoui's *The Beautiful Days Of Sheherazade* (1982) and Jilali Ferhati's *Reed Dolls* (1981), which tells the tragic story of a young girl forced into marriage, widowed while pregnant, and deprived of her children by the courts. Moroccan cinema has had an international outlet since the establishment of the annual Marrakech Film Festival in 2001.

SEE ALSO: Arabic literature; Festival and ceremony; French-language literature; Television and radio.

Rows of bicycles outside a movie theater in Marrakech, Morocco, testify to the enduring popularity of cinema. The annual film festival in this city has quickly become a major event, attracting big stars, and sponsorship from the Moroccan royal family.

MAJOR STYLES AND KEY PERFORMERS

Style	Artist	Country
Raï	Cheb Khaled	Algeria
Raï	Cheb Mami	Algeria
Kabylia (Berber) folk	Cheikh Nourredine	Algeria
Chaabi	Nass el-Ghiwane (band)	Morocco
Chaabi	Najat Aatabou	Morocco
Folk and contemporary	Khalil Farah	Sudan
Haqibah	Karoma	Sudan
Classical Oud	Anouar Brahem	Tunisia
Shaabi	Ahmed Adaweyah	Egypt
Shaabi	Hakim	Egypt
Al-Jil	Hamid el-Shaeri	Libya
Raï	Chaba Zahounia	Morocco

A street musician in Egypt with a traditional bowed instrument. There are many variations on this type of instrument in North Africa, including the fiddle-like rabab *and the Sudanese bow harp.*

THE MUSIC THAT IS PERFORMED TODAY IN NORTH AFRICA IS EXCEPTIONALLY DIVERSE, REFLECTING A CULTURAL CROSSROAD WHERE THE RICH FOLK TRADITIONS OF THE REGION, CLASSICAL ARAB MUSIC, AND WESTERN POPULAR MUSIC HAVE ALL MET AND BLENDED TOGETHER.

VARIED MUSICAL FORMS

North African music is enormously varied in style and form. There are three major musical threads that have played a key role in its development. These are the Berber, Arabic, and Andalusian classical traditions.

Berber folk music is the native musical form of the Maghreb (northwest Africa) and is best known in the Kabylia region of Algeria. It is also common in Morocco, Tunisia, and Libya. Traditional Berber instruments include the *rabab* (a one-stringed fiddle), the *lotar* (a lute, similar to the *guimbri* used by the Gnawa; see ORAL LITERATURE), hand drums, and bells. In the past, this folk music was composed to accompany group dances at religious ceremonies including circumcisions and coming-of-age rites. Berber people believe that their music and dance combine to generate a supernatural power that protects against evil spirits, misfortune, and even scorpion stings. Traditional Berber male folk musicians travel in groups of four, led by a poet (*amydaz*) and his counterpart, the clown figure or *bou oughanim*, who plays the double oboe. Other instruments in the quartet include the *rabab* and hand drums.

The second broad category of Maghrebi music is Middle Eastern in origin. Its many offshoots are practiced not only in North Africa, but throughout the Arab world. The first of these formal Arabic styles developed

Music was already a highly sophisticated art form in ancient Egypt. This mural from the Tomb of Nakht at Luxor shows a harpist (center). Harp, lute, and double oboe ensembles performed regularly at royal banquets.

in the seventh century, under the Umayyad dynasty in Syria, and spread from the eighth to the 13th centuries as Islam expanded across North Africa and into the Iberian peninsula (Spain and Portugal), where it maintained a foothold until 1492. Although it matured in the seventh century, Arabic classical music was subject to some far older influences, including Ancient Indian, Greek, and Semitic forms. The result was a style that displayed strong improvisational and rhythmic elements, employing a structure of *dum* (downbeats), *tak* (upbeats), and rests.

NONRELIGIOUS MUSIC AND SHARIA LAW

From the 1920s to the 1940s, Sudan's urban musicians were at the forefront of the campaign for Sudanese independence. Influential figures, such as the poet and singer Khalil Farah, challenged British control through their controversial lyrics and rebellious styles. During the second half of the 20th century, Sudanese music continued to innovate and experiment; traditional Arabic and African rhythms were blended with Jazz and Blues to produce new styles.

However, following the military coup of 1989 and the reintroduction of Islamic law (Sharia) by the National Islamic Front government, Sudan's official line on secular (nonreligious) music changed dramatically. It was seen as distracting people from their proper devotion to their religious duties, and was accused of promoting illicit sex and the consumption of alcohol. Accordingly, it was outlawed.

Today, secular music is heard only rarely in Sudan: in Church services in southern Sudan, in the refugee camps of northern Uganda, and among fighters of the Sudan People's Liberation Army (SPLA).

The final broad category of Maghrebi music is known as Andalusian classical. From the eighth century onward, when Spain (al-Andalus) came under Arab control, Córdoba in the south was one of the richest centers of Islamic classical music. When King Alfonso VIII had succeeded in driving the Arabs from most of southern Spain, this classical tradition spread throughout North Africa. The instruments of Andalusian classical include the *oud* (lute), *rabab* (fiddle), *qanun* (zither), *darbouka/doumbek* (goblet drums), *kamenjah* (violin), and *taarija* (tambourine). Variations on these instruments are found throughout the Arab world.

ANCIENT AND MODERN EGYPTIAN MUSIC

Documentary sources (including ancient texts and hieroglyphics) have shown that from as early as 3000 B.C.E. music was an integral part of religious and social life in Ancient Egypt. Even before this period, it is thought that percussion, stringed, and wind instruments were common. Percussion instruments included hand-held drums, castanets, bells, and the sistrum (a ceremonial rattle used in religious worship). Wind instruments included clarinets (single and twin-pipes), flutes and trumpets. Harps, lyres, and lutes comprised the early string

Musicians at a festival held in Ouargla in the Sahara desert in Algeria. The two musicians in the foreground are playing flutes, while behind them, a percussionist keeps time on a large tambourine-like instument called the bandair.

instruments mastered by musicians of the "Pharaonic" period.

The main style of Egyptian popular music, which is highly influential across the Arab World, is known as Shaabi (meaning "of the people"). Shaabi draws some inspiration from classical music, but owes more to Egyptian folk songs. It is a highly improvisational form of singing that often deals with themes of sadness and loss, but which can also be brash and comic. It developed in the poverty-stricken districts of Cairo following Egypt's demoralizing defeat by Israel in the Six-Day War of 1967. Ahmed Adaweyah was Egypt's first Shaabi superstar, who came to prominence in the 1970s. His songs were heavily censored by the Egyptian authorities because of their sexual content and their political message, which idealized the working class. Shaabi music is widely performed in nightclubs and at weddings and is particularly suitable for dancing with its fast and accelerating rhythms. Popular music is often played at weddings, particularly among working class communities, where it accompanies *raks sharki* or "bellydancing."

THE WORLD SACRED MUSIC FESTIVAL

This annual festival, held in the city of Fez in Morocco, seeks to unite musicians from around the world. The festival's organizers believe that music has a spiritual quality that enables it to overcome the political, economic, and cultural barriers that separate ethnic groups and nations. On this principle, many musicians and performers from around the world are invited to "share sacred music from the spiritual traditions of both East and West." The 2006 festival from May through June, on the theme "Paths of Hope," played host to acts and performances drawn from a great number of cultures and musical traditions. They range from Iraqi poetry to Afro-American gospel, and Amazonian ritual chanting to Pakistani Qawwali and Spanish Flamenco.

Al-Jil is another form of Egyptian and Libyan popular dance music that developed in the 1980s. Strongly influenced by Western trends, it is marketed to a younger audience and deals mainly with romantic themes.

MOROCCAN CHAABI

Chaabi is the name for the popular music of Morocco, which is widely performed at weddings and festivals. It is closely related to Egyptian Shaabi (Shaabi and Chaabi are the same word in Arabic). This dynamic and inventive style evolved out of the many forms of religious and folk music found in Morocco—including Berber, Sufi, and Gharnati—to become the music of the Moroccan soukh, or marketplace. Chaabi is often performed at street cafes in the evening, to the accompaniment of vigorous dancing and clapping.

As the Chaabi/Shaabi style spread throughout the Maghreb in the mid- to late 1970s, Western instruments like the electric guitar were adopted. Several influential Chaabi groups have emerged since this time. Their controversial song lyrics, dealing with themes such as government incompetence or social inequality, have often attracted censorship, and a number of Chaabi musicians have even been imprisoned.

ALGERIAN RAÏ

The Bedouins of the Oran region in Algeria are credited with laying the foundations of Raï music (which is also popular in Morocco). From the early 20th century onward, Bedouin musicians combined Spanish, French, African-American, and Arabic styles to create this new musical form, which literally translated means "way of seeing" or "opinion."

Raï has attracted criticism from more conservative elements in Algerian society due to its controversial lyrics, which often deal with subjects such as alcohol and sex. Islamist extremists issued death threats to

Raï artists, and in 1994–95 assassinated the young singer Cheb Hasni and the producer Rachid Baba-Ahmed. Yet Raï continued to enjoy huge success among young people, and from the 1980s onward gained worldwide fame through the recordings and performances of major stars such as Cheb Khaled, Cheb Mami, and Chaba Fadela. The masculine term *cheb* and its feminine form *chaba* both mean "young" and are often taken as a title by leading Raï singers.

SEE ALSO: *Arabs; Berbers; Dance and song; Festival and ceremony; Oral literature.*

Like most Raï singers, Cheb Khaled grew up in the port of Oran in Algeria. His passionate singing soon earned him the title "The King of Raï." He brought this musical style to world attention, but, under threat from extremists, he left his home country and settled in France.

FACT FILE

Population	Estimated at up to 1.4 million
Religion	Islam, Nuba religion, Christianity
Language	Various Nilo-Saharan and Arabic dialects.

TIMELINE

1500	Expansion of Kababish, Baggara, and Hamar nomads into the area surrounding the Nuba mountains.
1504	Establishment of Muslim Funj sultanate. Increasing Arabization and Islamization of northern Sudan.
c.1800	The Funj sultanate collapses.
1821	Turko-Egyptian conquest of the Sudan under Ibrahim Pasha.
1881–85	Mahdist revolution breaks out in the Sudan.
1882	British forces invade Egypt.
1889	British defeat Mahdists and establish Anglo-Egyptian government in Sudan.
1956	Sudan gains independence from Britain.
1962–72	First Sudanese civil war breaks out.
1983	Sharia (Islamic law) imposed by Khartoum government. Start of second Sudanese civil war; SPLA are active in the Nuba mountains.
2004	A peace deal is signed between the southern rebels and the Khartoum government. Special exceptions are made concerning the Nuba mountains.
2005	Southern rebels join the Sudanese government with SPLA leader John Garang as the new vice-president. Shortly after taking office, Garang is killed in a helicopter crash.

T HE NUBA ARE A DIVERSE GROUP MADE UP OF MORE THAN 50 DIFFERENT ETHNIC AND LOCAL GROUPINGS. LIVING IN THE NUBA MOUNTAINS IN SOUTHERN KORDOFAN, SUDAN, THEY HAVE IN RECENT TIMES SUFFERED ETHNIC CLEANSING BY THE SUDANESE GOVERNMENT.

HISTORY

Marking the point where the north and south of the Sudan meet, the Nuba mountains have experienced the comings and goings of many peoples. Each of these have had an influence on the make-up of the Nuba peoples and added to the complex cultural mix of the region. The term *Nuba* was coined by outsiders to distinguish the Black African hill dwellers of this area from the surrounding Arab peoples. It is an umbrella term that covers many distinct groups, such as the Heiban, Otoro, Tira, Moro, Korongo, Tullishi, Koalib, and Miri.

The linguistic diversity of the region is just as great as its cultural diversity, with a variety of dialects (local forms) of Nilo-Saharan, Bantu, and Arabic spoken. No single account can give a full picture of how and when the Nuba mountains were peopled, although the oral history of many groups recounts tales of their migrations into the area at various times in the past.

In recent decades the Nuba became caught up in Sudan's long-running civil war. As an enclave of black Africans within the predominantly Arab north of the country, many Nuba groups aligned themselves with the Sudanese People's Liberation Army

Young men dance at a festival, or sibir, *at Heiban in the Nuba mountains. The many* sibir *celebrated by the Nuba are associated with the seasons and are orchestrated by the village* kujur, *or rainmaker.*

(SPLA). Many Nuba combatants and civilians were killed, and thousands of people forcibly removed from their villages to government-run "peace camps." The status of the Nuba and their region was a major sticking point of the peace process (see box feature below).

SOCIETY AND DAILY LIFE

The Nuba's main livelihood is agriculture, supplemented by animal husbandry and hunting. Many Nuba peoples build agricultural terraces on steep slopes and practice limited irrigation with staple crops such as corn, bulrush millet, sorghum, and a variety of vegetables. Among most Nuba groups, agricultural land is owned by a male tribal head, who is free to dispense with the land as he sees fit. Generally a man's land is divided among his wives, who cultivate the land independently with the help of their own children.

AGE GRADES AND YOUTHFUL COMPETITION

The young men of the Tira, Otoro, and Moro peoples are initiated into a series of successive age grades. At around the age of 10 or 11 boys stop sleeping in their parents' home and move to the cattle camps to look after their fathers' herds. A year or so later the boys have their lower incisor teeth broken out so as to "help their growth." When aged 14 or 15, the boys pass into the first of four grades, each lasting three years. Each grade is associated with specific rights and responsibilities, as well as games and competitions. Novice grades take part in wrestling matches, while the two middle grades fight with sticks and shields. These sports are extremely competitive, with fierce inter-ethnic rivalries. Novices fear being held back an age grade if they do not perform well in these initiation tests.

Nuba social organization varies, with some groups practicing matrilineal descent (that is, through the mother's line) and others patrilineal descent (through the father's). In the past, Nuba society was mostly based around the clan (several families linked by a common ancestor). So-called "big men" held authority based on personal qualities of strength, oratory, diplomacy, or wealth, but their positions were temporary and could not be passed on through the family. With colonialism a more formal system of local sheikhs (chiefs) was put in place. Nuba social organization was drastically disrupted by the civil war, as a result of forcible conscription and displacement.

Nuba women collecting firewood and water. Women share the tasks of crop growing and animal herding with men, and also fought in the civil war.

(Right) This young Nuba boy's drawing of a soldier with a rocket-propelled grenade testifies to the ferocity of the war in the Nuba mountains. Government forces sealed off the area and attempted genocide against the Nuba.

CULTURE AND RELIGION

From the 16th century the Nuba mountains came increasingly under the influence of Islamic nomads and the Funj sultanate. Many Nuba are Muslim, although particular groups have assimilated Islam in different ways. For example, the Miri observe certain fundamental aspects of Islam, such as belief in the one God and Muslim marriage and funeral rites. However, they do not adhere strictly to regular daily prayer, fasting during the holy month of Ramadan, or the prohibition against drinking alcohol.

The Miri also practice preexisting religious rites alongside Islam. For example, they have kept several pre-Islamic harvest festivals, at which rain priests (*kujur*) perform. They also consult priestly oracles, special shamans who are possessed by spirits and prophesy the good and bad fortunes of the village. The Miri regard these ceremonies as preserving the natural order ordained by Allah and professed in the Quran, and not as contradicting Islam.

A minority of Nuba, living in the south of the mountains, are Christians.

SEE ALSO: *Arabs; Baggara; Dinka; Festival and ceremony; Shilluk.*

THE NUBA AND THE CIVIL WAR

During the colonial period, the British divided the huge territory of the Sudan into a number of provinces, which were retained after independence in 1956. The northern provinces are inhabited by mainly Arab, Arabic-speaking, and Muslim peoples, while those in the south are peopled predominantly by black Africans who practice Christianity or preexisting religions. The second Sudanese civil war that broke out in 1983 was primarily based on this north–south divide. The Nuba were in an odd position—their homeland was traditionally part of the north, though as black Africans they supported the southern cause and so came into violent conflict with their Islamic neighbors, the Baggara. In the peace talks of 2002–04 the Nuba Mountains region was claimed by both sides, and so was made subject to a special power-sharing agreement to allay Nuba fears that they would suffer further reprisals and human rights violations. The situation is further complicated by the presence of oil reserves in the Nuba Mountains.

FACT FILE

Population	Nubians are thought to number well over 500,000, with more than 300,000 in Egypt and at least 200,000 in Sudan.
Religion	Islam; pre-Islamic religious practices
Language	Nubian (Nilotic), local Arabic dialects.

TIMELINE

c.2500 B.C.E.	Nubian kingdom begins to take shape at Kerma near the Third Cataract of the Nile.
750 B.C.E.	Newly formed kingdom of Kush based at Napata near the Fourth Cataract pushes north into Egypt to found the 25th Dynasty.
656 B.C.E.	Kush loses control of Egypt.
c.300 B.C.E.	Center of Kushite power relocates south to Meroë.
c.550 C.E.	Christian kingdoms are established in Nubia.
641	Arab forces invade Egypt.
651	Muslim Egypt and Christian Nubia sign a treaty.
c.1250	Nubian Christian kingdoms begin to disintegrate or fall under Muslim rule.
1504–1800	The Funj sultanate dominates southern Nubia.
1821	Turko-Egyptian forces conquer Sudan.
1881–85	Mahdist revolution takes place in Sudan.
1898	British defeat Mahdists and establish Anglo-Egyptian government in Sudan.
1956	Sudan wins independence from Britain and Egypt.
1963	Building of Aswan High Dam floods Lower Nubia.
2004	Merowe Dam construction near the Fourth Cataract causes further displacement of Nubian people.

THE REGION KNOWN HISTORICALLY AS NUBIA COVERS A STRETCH OF THE NILE VALLEY FROM ASWAN IN SOUTHERN EGYPT TO DONGOLA IN THE SUDAN. CIVILIZATIONS FIRST AROSE THERE SOME 5,000 YEARS AGO. MANY MODERN NUBIANS HAVE BEEN DISPLACED FROM THEIR ORIGINAL HOMELAND, BUT HAVE RETAINED PARTS OF THEIR ANCIENT CULTURE.

HISTORY

Nubia came successively under the control of ancient Egypt, the Christian Byzantine empire, and Muslim Arabs. The Nubians have therefore long influenced, and been influenced by, different cultures and peoples.

From the sixth century C.E., Nubia was home to Christian kingdoms that flourished for several centuries, building beautifully decorated churches and monasteries. They were able to maintain their independence from Muslim control until the migration of Arabic-speaking livestock herders and attacks by the Mamluke rulers of Egypt in the 13th and 14th centuries led to their collapse and a gradual conversion of the population to Islam. In 1504 African invaders from either the White Nile region or Ethiopia overran parts of Nubia and, converting to Islam, founded the Funj sultanate at Sennar on the Blue Nile. Funj dominance over much of upper Nubia accelerated the Arabization of the region. However, Nilotic Nubian dialects persisted in more northerly areas. Today most Nubians speak Arabic dialects, often with some elements of older Nubian languages.

Whitewashed adobe (mud-brick) houses in a Nubian village near Aswan, Egypt. The vaulted roofs with ventilation holes are a traditional architectural feature of this region.

ANCIENT NUBIA

Nubia was well known throughout the ancient world as the source of such precious commodities as ivory and slaves. Through this trade the rulers of Nubia developed a unique civilization that blended Egyptian and Nubian elements. Known as Kush, ancient Nubia was powerful enough by 720 B.C.E. to conquer Egypt and found its 25th Dynasty. While the Nubians were only to rule Egypt for a short period, their culture continued to flourish, reaching its zenith during the third to first centuries B.C.E. The later capital of the ancient Nubians at Meroë on the Upper Nile testifies to the skill and creativity of these people. Meroë's ruins include more than 50 pyramidal tombs, and unique hieroglyphic inscriptions. Meroitic civilization declined in the first to the third centuries C.E. and was eventually destroyed by invaders from the Axumite kingdom of Ethiopia. Yet the achievements of the ancient Nubians remain one of Africa's greatest cultural legacies, and continue to influence modern life on the Upper Nile to the present day.

Model figures of 40 Nubian archers from the Egyptian 11th dynasty (2125–1985 B.C.E.). During this turbulent period in Egyptian history, many Nubian mercenaries served in Upper Egypt.

SOCIETY AND DAILY LIFE

Rural Nubians are crop-growing farmers. Before they were displaced by the building of the Aswan High Dam in 1963–70, they relied on the Nile to sustain their crops. The river's annual flooding deposited small amounts of fertile alluvial soils, which were used to grow wheat, sorghum, millet, date palms, and vegetables. Nubians used various water-lifting devices to irrigate their fields, including the ancient shaduf, a counterweighted bucket on a pole.

Nubian men work in the fields while women tend the livestock, clean grain, and do domestic chores. Since 1983 the imposition of strict Islamic law by the Sudanese government has heavily restricted the role of women. For example, women are expected to cover themselves and to avoid contact with unknown men by remaining in the household compound.

The 20th century witnessed the migration of many Nubians to the urban centers of Egypt and Sudan. There they formed large communities and found success in all walks of life. As is the case in most rural African communities, migrant work is also common and many Nubian families rely, at least in part, on wages sent to them from urban areas. In 1963 more than 90,000 Nubians were relocated to make way for construction of the Aswan High Dam (see box feature).

CULTURE AND RELIGION

While Nubians today are Muslim, many remnants of Nubia's pre-Islamic past are still apparent in its culture. Traditions such as bed burial on native *angareb* beds are a modified form of a practice that existed in the ancient Nubian Meroitic kingdom. Similarly, facial scarification, involving three vertical cuts on each cheek (though now only practiced by the older generation), can be seen on stone-carved temple reliefs from Meroë. Traditions with Christian roots include an emphasis on matrilineal descent (that is, through the mother), the drawing of a cross on the head of newborn babies, the use of palm fronds and fish bones to make ritual objects, and the custom of bathing in the Nile on ceremonial occasions. An interesting recent cultural development is the growth of the Zar cult among some Nubian women. Followers of this cult—who often have troubled home lives—dance to drive away evil spirits. The purifying ritual that the women perform strengthens them and helps them challenge the male dominance in strict Islamic society.

SEE ALSO: Arabs; Islam; Nuba.

Nubian women transporting goods on Lake Nasser. Around 45 Nubian villages were submerged when this, the world's largest artificial lake, was created. Most people were relocated near the town of Aswan.

NUBIA AND THE ASWAN DAM

Completed in 1970, the Aswan High Dam created a giant reservoir, Lake Nasser, and displaced some 90,000 Nubian villagers. The Egyptian Nubians were resettled at Kom Ombo north of the modern town of Aswan, while the Sudanese Nubians were dispersed to distant locations. The building of the Dam not only forced thousands of people to leave their original homelands, but also destroyed many sites of historical and cultural interest. Many Nubian homes, which were characterized by their unique, colorful architecture, were lost forever, while the impressive temple of Abu Simbel from the time of the pharaohs was rebuilt in a new location. The relocated Nubians were forced to adjust to an entirely new existence. Many migrated to large urban centers, though even in these changed circumstances (in Egypt, at least) their culture continues to thrive. Indeed, Nubian culture has undergone a renaissance since the early 1970s; Nubians proud of their cultural identity have revived many traditional crafts, leading to Aswan being named UNESCO City of Folk Art in 2005.

FACT FILE

Population	There are thought to be up to 1.4 million Nuer in Sudan, with some 40,000 in refugee camps in Ethiopia.
Religion	Christianity, Preexisting religions
Language	Nuer dialects are widely intelligible to the Dinka, and together they form a sub-branch of the Western River–Lake branch of the Nilotic language group.

TIMELINE

3000–2000 B.C.E.	Cattle keepers speaking an early form of Western Nilotic are resident in southern Sudan.
c.1000	Nilotic peoples settled in region to the far southwest of the Bahr al Ghazal river.
c.1700s	Nuer people begin to migrate eastward.
1818–90	Nuer expand east of the Nile to the Ethiopian border.
1821	Trade routes opened up from north to south Sudan; southern population reduced by slavery and disease.
1842	First European explorers reach Nuerland.
1870–73	British governor Samuel Baker tries to annex the Upper Nile for the Khedive of Egypt and eradicate slave trade.
1900–1930s	British military expeditions against the Nuer.
1920s	Christian missionary schools established in Nuerland.
1956	Sudan wins independence from Britain and Egypt.
1962–72	First Sudanese civil war takes place.
1983	Sharia (Islamic law) imposed by Khartoum government, sparking the second Sudanese civil war.
1991	Nuer–Dinka split in the SPLA.
2004	SPLA leader John Garang signs peace agreement with Khartoum government.

ALONGSIDE THEIR CLOSE RELATIVES THE DINKA, THE NILOTIC-SPEAKING NUER LIVE IN THE EXTENSIVE MARSHLANDS OF THE UPPER NILE IN SOUTHERN SUDAN. CATTLE-KEEPING ANCESTORS OF THESE PEOPLES ARE THOUGHT TO HAVE COLONIZED WHAT IS NOW SOUTHERN SUDAN AS EARLY AS 3000–2000 B.C.E.

HISTORY

The oral history of the Nuer and written records going back to the early 1800s record a great expansion of their territory at that time. This period of growth, which absorbed several other peoples, was largely at the expense of the Dinka. Later in the 19th century the Nuer put up fierce resistance to colonial rule, which resulted in the Nuer and the Dinka being separated and a series of British military expeditions. After Sudanese independence in 1956, the Nuer were active in both the first civil war (1962–72) and the second civil war (1983–2004). In 1991 senior Nuer members of the Sudanese People's Liberation Army (SPLA) called for the overthrow of John Garang, the SPLA's Dinka leader. This caused a factional split within the SPLA that eventually provoked bloody Nuer–Dinka fighting, which has only recently been resolved.

SOCIETY AND DAILY LIFE

Sudan's devastating civil wars have severely disrupted Nuer traditional life. Much of the population has experienced life within refugee camps, either in the Sudan or in Ethiopia, while many (including children)

A traditional Nuer dwelling on the banks of the White Nile in Sudan. The Nuer do not have any system of central authority and refer to themselves simply as Naath, *or "human beings."*

have been drawn into the military conflict. A significant number of Nuer now live in Khartoum's squatter camps.

Prewar Nuer life revolved around the seasonal cycle. During the wet season major flooding makes it necessary to retreat to villages on higher ground, where corn and sorghum were grown and fish caught. During the dry season the cattle were taken out to pasture and temporary cattle camps established. Cattle play an important symbolic role in bridewealth transactions (gifts by the bridegroom to the bride's family) and various ritual sacrifices.

The Nuer are not ruled by chiefs or kings. Rather, they are organized into many clans, which comprise 11 major territorial groupings. Historically these groups acted independently and were often in conflict with each other. Yet they would unite against threats from neighboring groups such as the Dinka and Shilluk. The guiding principle of the Nuer social system is neatly summarized in the old Arab saying: "me and my brother against each other; me and my brother against my cousins; me and my cousins against the world."

CATTLE AND THE NUER

Cattle are central to the Nuer way of life. They are the most valuable possessions of Nuer men, who will defend their herds with their lives. The livestock have a practical purpose, supplying communities with milk and meat. Cattle are owned by the head of the family; they are herded by the men but milked by the women. Cattle also have an enormous social significance: a person's prestige is measured by how many head of cattle the family possesses and the quality of the individual animals. Up to 40 cattle may be presented as gifts by the bridegroom to the bride's family upon marriage. Cattle are the source of most conflicts between clans, but are also the means by which such conflicts are resolved; fines for offenses caused by one group to another are paid in the form of cattle. Because the Nuer believe that cows are possessed by the ghost of their owner's ancestors, they are often ritually sacrificed in religious ceremonies to allow people to establish contact with the spirits. The Nuer have 12 different words to describe the common variations in color and coat patterning among their cattle. People often take the name of their favorite cow or bull as their own nickname.

CULTURE AND RELIGION

Although the Nuer believe in a single God, Kwoth ("spirit"), to whom they pray and make sacrifices, various lesser spirits (*kuth*) are actually more important in their daily lives, having the power to bring both fortune and misfortune. The Nuer make offerings of livestock to the *kuth*, particularly during significant rites of passage, such as weddings and initiations. The Nuer also accord great importance to the ritual role of the so-called "leopard-skin priest." The priest's main historical function was to act as a mediator between parties in a blood feud (a homicide). In more recent times, these priests came to be associated with prophecy. During the 19th and 20th centuries, a number of influential prophets emerged who, drawing

The civil war that affected the south of Sudan for more than 20 years (1983–2005) displaced thousands of people and disrupted many communities. Aid agencies are focusing on education to bring hope for the future. Here, a class of young Nuer men assemble at an outdoor school.

their authority from possession by spirits, became charismatic popular leaders at times of crisis. Some, such as the prophet Ngungdeng, who united the Nuer in their struggle against British rule, even had significant monuments of adobe and ivory erected in their honor. Since the 1920s, the Nuer have been greatly influenced by the work of Christian missionaries and many preexisting Nuer beliefs have been amalgamated with Christian ones. Yet Nuer ideas of spirit possession and prophecy remain important.

In the past the Nuer wore very few clothes. Nuer women were adorned with beaded headdresses and necklaces. Nuer men, on the other hand, were readily identifiable by the six scars that were cut across their forehead as part of their initiation. Nuer men were also circumcized and inducted into a named group of their peers known as an age set. However, these customs are becoming less common.

SEE ALSO: *Arabs; Dinka, Shilluk.*

THE NUER–DINKA CONFLICT
During the second Sudanese civil war (1983–2005), conflict erupted between the Nuer and Dinka. The immediate causes of the fighting were cattle raiding and kidnapping of people. However, many observers claimed that the Sudanese government was behind the trouble, arming both sides in a "divide and rule" policy to try and secure the oil wealth of the south of the country. The government put out propaganda about "slavery" being conducted by these peoples. In 1999, from February to March, the Dinka–Nuer West Bank Peace and Reconciliation Conference was organized by the New Sudan Council of Churches to bring the two sides together and end the years of bitter conflict.

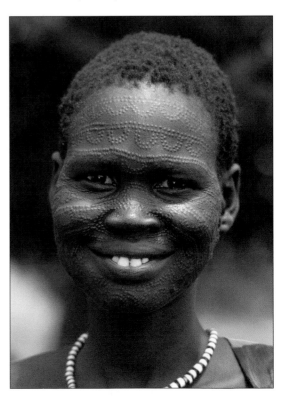

Nuer people of both sexes, such as this young girl, have long had the custom of decorating their faces and bodies with elaborate scarring ("scarification").

EXAMPLES OF ORAL LITERATURE

In the **Beginning of Agriculture** legend told by the Kabyles of Algeria, the first man and woman are wandering under the earth and see an ant storing grain. The woman urges the man to kill the ant but he refuses. Instead they begin questioning the ant, which leads them to the earth's surface and teaches them all the basic skills they need to stay alive, including making fire, sowing grain, and making bread.

The **Sirat al-Sultan Baybars** (Life of Sultan Baybars) is a popular tale throughout the Arab world, recounting the heroic exploits of the first Mamluke ruler of Egypt.

The Dinka of southern Sudan have a huge stock of folktales and songs, including the legend **Atong**, about a woman who ignores her brothers' advice and unwisely marries a lion. Many Dinka stories have been collected by the Sudanese scholar and diplomat Francis Mading Deng in his book *Dinka Folktales* (1974).

NORTH AFRICA HAS A LONG TRADITION OF WRITING, AND MANY ANCIENT STORIES AND MYTHS HAVE BEEN PRESERVED IN WRITTEN FORM. YET WRITING WAS LONG THE PRESERVE OF SPECIALISTS. AMONG THE WIDER POPULATION, ORAL FOLK LITERATURE BECAME A HIGHLY SKILLED ART, IN WHICH PROFESSIONAL STORYTELLERS RECOUNTED AND EMBELLISHED POPULAR TALES.

HISTORY

Some of the earliest folk tales of the region are myths that tell of the creation of a particular people or recount the origins of their culture. For example, the Kabyles, a Berber group from the Djurdjura mountains on the coast of Algeria, have a legend that explains the origins of agriculture. In this, an ant shows the first people how to grow wheat and grind it into flour, and then how to light a fire and bake the dough into bread.

Most oral literature of North Africa takes its origins from the earliest known Arabic tales and poems of the seventh to eighth centuries C.E. The structure of the Arabic language is well suited to harmonious word

Storytelling and musical performance often go hand in hand (above). Here, a storyteller in the city of Fez, Morocco, accompanies his tale with tunes on a wooden flute.

The telling of folktales is a traditional pastime among the nomadic Bedouin of North Africa and Arabia (left). Gathered around a campfire, Bedouin men smoke their hookah water pipes and recount stories.

patterns with complex rhythms and rhymes. The traditional poem of this early period is the *qasidah* (ode), which normally consists of 70 to 80 pairs of half-lines. *Qasidah* commonly describe nomadic life, including romances and tales of journeys and great hardships. Later styles include the *sirah* ("life" or "biography") which is often based on a historical character. One of the most famous told in North Africa is the greatly embellished tale of Baybars I (1223–77), the first Mamluke ruler of Egypt and Syria. The tale portrays Baybars as a people's champion fighting against bureaucracy and tyranny. The underdog triumphing against oppression is a common theme in Arab storytelling.

Much North African oral literature was collected by French scholars during the colonial period. This body of knowledge provides an insight into the peoples of the region. Unfortunately, much of this literature has not been widely studied, particularly in the English-speaking world.

ORAL LITERATURE TODAY

As in much of the rest of the world, the spread of the written word has brought a decline in the number of stories that are

The Arabic world has a rich fund of folktales. Jama' al-Fna square in Marrakech, Morocco (above) is famous as a place where professional storytellers gather to perform such tales.

remembered and transmitted by oral means alone. However, professional urban storytellers can still be found in some parts of the region. Perhaps the best-known public space where such entertainers gather and perform is the large open market square in the Moroccan city of Marrakech known as the Jama' al-Fna.

In more rural parts of North Africa oral stories remain important. The nomadic Bedouin of Egypt's Nile delta are especially famed for their oral verse recited from memory. Such poetry is used to express strong feelings of love, sadness, and anger, which are otherwise seen as socially inappropriate. Similarly, among the rural Berbers of Morocco, oral "tales of wonder" are common. These tales are primarily recounted by women and are passed down from mothers to their daughters. Their aim is to teach girls what the socially acceptable forms of behavior are for women. They therefore include tales of obedient girls, evil stepmothers, and jealous cowives. At one level, these stories conform to a male-dominated view of the world, yet at another level they hint at resistance and nonconformity. Thus, some stories that have daring, "bad" girls as their central characters hint at the ways in which women can react and fight against male domination.

The Gnawa of Morocco are a mystical brotherhood of black Muslims who use music and storytelling as a way of healing. Members of this religious caste are descendents of slaves who were brought to the Maghreb (coastal North Africa) from West Africa during the time of the trans-Saharan slave trade. Their tales and songs reflected and helped them heal the pain and misery of their captivity—much like the development of the Blues among African-Americans. Gnawa performances today are not just for entertainment but have a social and spiritual role as well; their skills are reputed to cure insanity and help people escape evil influences. The trance ceremonies, known as *derbela*, during which the healing takes place are held at night usually last until morning.

DINKA FOLKTALES

While much of the oral literature of North Africa comes from an Arab and Islamic cultural background, the peoples of the southern Sudan, such as the Dinka, Nuer, and Shilluk, represent a different cultural tradition that draws upon an equally intricate and deep-rooted body of myth. Perhaps the most extensive body of oral literature from the southern Sudan was collected by the Dinka scholar Francis Mading Deng (b.1938) and can be found in his book *Dinka Folktales* (1974). These tales cover a wide variety of topics, including myths of creation and leadership, tales of morality, and tales explaining the characteristics of the natural world, particularly the attributes of various animals. The Dinka are adept at using complex metaphors and, rather like Aesop's Fables, they tend to make comparisons between people and animals, using such stories to point out human failings. For example, a popular Dinka tale readily accessible to Western readers relates the story of the Fox and his trickery.

SEE ALSO: *Arabic literature; Arabs; Berbers; Dance and song; Dinka; Islam; Music and musical instruments.*

SCULPTURE

SINCE ANCIENT TIMES, THE PEOPLES OF NORTH AFRICA HAVE CREATED SCULPTURES USING A WIDE VARIETY OF MATERIALS, SUCH AS STONE, CLAY, METALS, IVORY, AND WOOD. TODAY, SCULPTURE IS STILL THRIVING AS AN ART FORM ACROSS THE REGION.

HISTORY

The ancient Egyptians were well known for their magnificent, monumental works of art. Prominent among these are their great sculptures in stone, such as the Sphinx or the statues at the Temple of Amun in Karnak. The Egyptians generally followed a strict set of rules when carving three-dimensional sculptures, and works of art were not meant to be true to life in their shape or form. Rather, they were designed to perform a highly

symbolic function, emphasizing important characteristics and showing the position of characters within Egyptian life. For example, the ancient Egyptians used the relative size of figures on their sculptures to symbolize the different ranks of people in their social order. Accordingly, the pharaoh was portrayed as larger than life, while high-ranking officials were shown life-size. Peasants were depicted as small figures, and

One of the most famous stone sculptures in the world is the Sphinx, which stands near the pyramids at Giza. This mysterious figure, with a human head and a lion's body, was made in around 2500 B.C.E.

were often shown performing menial tasks. In its form, Egyptian sculpture nearly always echoed the shape of the stone block from which it was fashioned. The front of almost every ancient Egyptian statue is the most important aspect, as the figure sits or stands facing rigidly forward.

SCULPTURE TODAY

Since the seventh century C.E., much North African sculpture has been increasingly influenced by Arab and Islamic art. Islam forbids the representation of people and other living beings as an arrogant attempt to mimic creative powers that belong solely to Allah. Instead, Islamic sculpture takes the form of geometric carvings and calligraphy incorporated into architectural features or ornate furnishings. In Morocco wooden carvings have been particularly important for many centuries. Although it is now becoming rare, the wood of the cedar trees that grew in the central region of the Atlas mountains was widely used, since it lent itself well to carving. Cedar also has the advantages of being fragrant and resistant to decay. Architecturally, wooden sculptures were used as roof supports and ornamental details such as canopy columns, lintels, corbels (supporting brackets), inscribed friezes, and decorative illustrations on doors and ceilings. Of particular artistic note are the intricately sculpted (and sometimes painted) doors of buildings in the High Atlas mountains.

Among the peoples of southern Sudan there is a variety of very different sculpting traditions. In this region, figures that resemble human beings are common, with wood, and sometimes clay, being the primary media. The creation of ornate ceramic vessels may be seen as an artistic form of sculpture in its own right, particularly among seminomadic peoples who must combine artistic endeavor with practical functionality.

This carved door (right) is from the the abandoned kasbah (walled citadel) of Telouet in the High Atlas mountains of Morocco. The intricately decorated doors and ceilings of this and other kasbahs in the region are made from the local Atlas cedar tree.

Of particular interest are the ceramic figures created by the children of peoples who live around the Nile in southern Sudan, such as the Nuer and the Dinka. These small sculptures generally take the form of cattle with elaborately shaped horns decorated with tassels (although human figures and other wild animals are also common). Since livestock play a central role in the lives of these Nilotic peoples, the small clay sculptures have an educational function. The children use them as toys to act out the daily life of the adult herders, looking forward to a time when they will have cattle of their own.

SEE ALSO: *Architecture; Calligraphy; Dinka; Islam; Nuer.*

The top of a Bongo sculpture (left), which once marked the grave of a hunter. These memorial carvings were made from mahogany. Since this hardwood is resistant to rot and termite attack, the sculptures—many of which are thought to be up to 120 years old—have been well preserved.

BONGO GRAVE SCULPTURES

Some of southern Sudan's most celebrated art forms are the grave sculptures of the Bongo and Belanda peoples, who lived by hunting up until the early 1970s. When a Bongo hunter died, a number of wooden sculptures were put up around the burial mound containing his grave. These sculptures took the form of wooden poles, with intricately carved shafts and a stylized human head or figure at the top. Hollowed-out, bowl-shaped rings around the shaft symbolize the preparation of hunting medicine, while spherical carvings represent the heads of game animals that the hunter has killed. The heads on top of the poles may represent the hunter himself or refer to the people he has slain. The number and shape of these funerary monuments depended on the acts performed by the dead person. In particular, they related to his hunting prowess and the number of feasts of merit that he was able to give. In recent years these sculptures have become highly prized among Western collectors.

SHILLUK

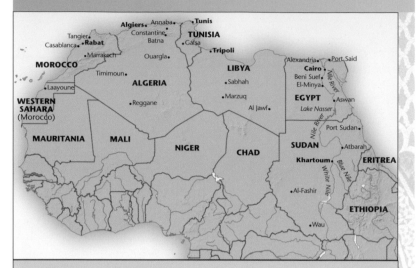

FACT FILE

Population	Estimates of the size of the Shilluk population are difficult to find. Early in the 20th century they numbered some 100,000 and are likely to have grown in size since then. It is thought that they may now number around 600,000.
Religion	Christianity, Shilluk religion
Language	The Shilluk are a Western (River–Lake) Nilotic speaking people, most closely related to the Luo of southern Sudan and eastern Uganda and the Nuer and Dinka of southern Sudan.

TIMELINE

c.1500	Shilluk diverge from the Luo and migrate to their present homeland, possibly from Lake Victoria. The Shilluk nation is established by Nyikang.
1684	Shilluk carry out attacks on Arab settlements.
1842	First European explorers reach Shillukland.
1889–1956	Sudan under Anglo-Egyptian government.
1918	Investiture of the 29th Shilluk king, Fafiti Yor.
1943	Death of Fafiti Yor; the 30th king, Anei, ascends the throne but dies in 1944.
1962–72	First Sudanese civil war takes place.
1983	Sharia (Islamic law) imposed by Khartoum government, sparking the second Sudanese civil war. Shilluk support the Sudanese People's Liberation Army.
1989	Over 700 Shilluk are massacred by government militia at Jebelein.
1993	Kwango Dak Pudiet ascends the Shilluk throne.
2005	Peace agreement ends the second Sudanese civil war.

THE SHILLUK INHABIT A CONTINUOUS STRETCH ALONG THE WESTERN BANK OF THE UPPER NILE IN SUDAN. TO THE SOUTH OF THEIR HOMELAND ARE THE NUER AND DINKA, THOUGH THE SHILLUK ARE FEWER IN NUMBER THAN THEIR NEIGHBORS.

HISTORY

Shilluk legends recount how their present site of occupation was settled by the first king, Nyikang, some 31 generations ago (c.1500–1600). In modern times, the Shilluk were, like the other ethnic groups of southern Sudan, caught up in the civil war that raged until 2005. In 1989 some 700 Shilluk farm laborers were massacred by Arab milita in the village of Jebelein, north of Kodok. In 2004 Shilluk villages were attacked again from February through May, leaving more than 100 people dead.

SOCIETY AND DAILY LIFE

The Shilluk are settled agriculturalists who keep far fewer cattle than the Nuer and Dinka. Shilluk land is dotted with hamlets, each of which is made up of a few individual homesteads grouped around a common cattle byre. Hamlets are arranged into clusters of settlements and each settlement has a dominant family line (known as a *diel*) from which a chief is drawn. Shilluk territory is further divided into two ceremonial halves, north and south, each with a paramount chief who together elect new kings from the royal lineages. Shilluk kingship was outlawed by the British but restored on independence in 1956. The present *reth* (king) was invested in 1993.

Shilluk men and women celebrate the investiture of their king, Kwango Dak Pudiet, in 1993. Every Shilluk king is believed to be a reincarnation of the original reth, *Nyikang.*

CULTURE AND RELIGION

The Shilluk believe in a single creator god (Juok), but the central figure in their belief system is their first legendary king Nyikang. The spirit of Nyikang is thought to be present in each successive king, who holds power over war, fertility, health, crops, and animals. The king's well-being is intimately linked to the prosperity of the whole nation. A number of shrines are dedicated to Nyikang. They comprise a circular fenced enclosure and several large traditional huts, which are maintained by a priestly caste.

SEE ALSO: Arabs; Dinka; Nuer.

CROWNING THE NEW KING

The coronation of a new king is an elaborate affair that reaffirms the political structure of the Shilluk territory. A few days after a king dies the paramount chiefs of the north and south gather with other important chiefs and appoint one of the royal princes as the new king (a king usually has many sons from many wives). About a year later the coronation takes place; all groups within Shilluk society are required to provide certain essential objects for this ceremony, such as ostrich feathers, spears, drums, cowrie shells, and livestock for sacrifice. A model of Nyikang is then brought down from the north of the country and a series of mock battles ensues between Nyikang at the head of a northern army and the king-elect, who leads an army from the south. Eventually Nyikang captures the chosen king and holds him prisoner before passing into him as a spirit. Once this has taken place, Nyikang and the new king are united in the office of kingship and the two halves of the country are also symbolically reunited.

MAJOR BROADCASTING ORGANIZATIONS

Country	Broadcasters	Ownership/Control
Algeria	Enterprise Nationale de Télévision	State
	BRTV	Private (External broadcaster)
	Algerian Radio	State
Egypt	Egypt Radio Television Union	State
	Nile TV International	State
	Dream TV	Private
	Al-Mihwar TV	Private
	Nile FM	Private
	Nogoum FM	Private
Libya	Great Jamahiryah TV & Radio	State
	Voice of Africa	State (External broadcaster)
Morocco	Radio-Télévision Marocaine	State
	2M	State
	Medi 1	Private
Sudan	Sudan National Broadcasting Corporation	State
	Sudan National Radio Corporation	State
	Mango 96 FM	Private
	Voice of Hope	Illegal
	Voice of Sudan	Illegal
Tunisia	Tunisian Radio & Television Establishment	State
	Hannibal TV	Private
	Tunisian Radio	State
	Radio Mosaique	Private

Radio and television have now spread widely across North Africa. In the remote Egyptian Sinai desert, a Bedouin camel rider carries a portable radio on his saddlebag. Satellite technology is bringing television into ever more homes and communities.

NORTH AFRICA IS QUITE WELL SERVED BY RADIO AND TELEVISION. SOME COUNTRIES HAVE DEVELOPED A MAJOR BROADCAST INDUSTRY THAT IS RECEIVED BY A WIDE AUDIENCE ACROSS THE REGION. HOWEVER, CENSORSHIP IS STILL WIDESPREAD. SINCE THE 1990S, THE NUMBER OF PRIVATE BROADCASTERS HAS GROWN, INCREASING CHOICE AND DIVERSITY OF OPINION.

STATE CONTROL AND CENSORSHIP

State control and censorship of North African broadcast media by national governments remains strong throughout the region, though it varies greatly from state to state. Television and radio stations in Egypt, Algeria, Morocco, and Tunisia are relatively free to criticize the government, although in all of these countries a broadcaster can be penalized with a prison sentence or a hefty fine for reports attacking politicians, Islam, and the military (or, in Morocco, the monarchy). In Algeria extremists of the GIA (Group Islamique Armée, or Armed Islamic Group) have assassinated several journalists. Broadcast media in Sudan and Libya are far more strictly controlled and government approves almost all radio and television output. International organizations have criticized Sudan for maintaining one of the most repressive broadcast regimes in Africa.

Broadcasting is also used as a way of resisting oppressive state authority. In Sudan a number of illegal and clandestine radio stations operate, such as the National Democratic Alliance's "Voice of Sudan" and the Christian station "Voice of Hope." A radio station in Western Sahara, a disputed territory claimed by Morocco, supports the Polisario Front independence movement.

SOCIAL IMPLICATIONS

The impact of mass media, and especially television, is to open up any region to influences and ideas from all over the world. Programs from Egypt, which is by far the most prolific television broadcaster in North Africa, are seen throughout the Arab world, which has resulted in a growing use of Egyptian Arabic in other Arab countries. Since it is fairly liberal in comparison to many other Islamic countries, Egyptian television also challenges conservative Islamic values by showing women wearing non-traditional dress and in non-traditional roles. By contrast, in Sudan strict Islamic Sharia law prohibits women from being seen in any public context whatsoever.

SEE ALSO: Islam; Movies.

Customers in an Egyptian cafe watching a soccer match. Sport is a major draw; the African Nations Cup soccer tournament, held in Tunisia in 2004, attracted large television audiences across the region.

NILESAT 101 AND 102

Egypt has taken the lead in adopting new broadcasting technologies, becoming the first country in Africa to acquire its own satellite with the launch of Nilesat 101 on April 25, 1998. The satellite, which was launched into space by a French Ariane rocket, was part of a project begun in 1995 by President Hosni Mubarak at a total cost of U.S.$170 million. Nilesat 101 broadcast 100 digital television channels, which were received across North Africa by an estimated 5 million households. In 2000, the more advanced Nilesat 102 was launched, which is capable of broadcasting 150 digital television channels, as well as providing internet capabilities. Egypt's pioneering work in telecommunications technologies has strengthened its dominant cultural influence over other North African Arabic-speaking nations.

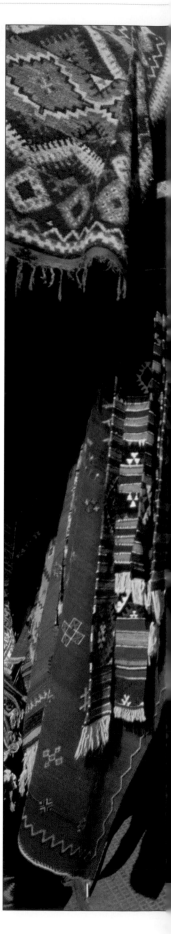

ORTH AFRICA HAS A LONG HISTORY OF TEXTILE PRODUCTION IN BOTH LINEN AND WOOL DATING TO THE TIME OF THE ANCIENT EGYPTIANS. EGYPTIAN LONG-STAPLE COTTON IS STILL RENOWNED AS A FINE FABRIC. BUT PERHAPS THE MOST FAMOUS TEXTILES MADE IN THE REGION TODAY ARE WOVEN WOOLEN CARPETS AND RUGS.

HISTORY

From the earliest times the ancient Egyptians were skilled weavers and, due to the dry conditions in many Egyptian tombs, numerous examples of textiles from this period have been preserved. Some of the most famous textiles were recovered from the tomb of Tutankhamun, and include an ornate linen tunic now in the Egyptian Museum in Cairo. From the third century C.E. on designs made by the Coptic Christian community became

popular in Egypt. These weaves were influenced by designs that had originally been popular in Ancient Greece and Byzantium (Constantinople), including detailed plant and animal symbols.

With the coming of the Islamic period, Coptic designs were gradually replaced by Arabic inscriptions and geometric patterns. Under Arab rulers the textile industry became a palace institution and fine textiles served as important markers of prestige and status. By the end of the 11th century Egyptian towns such as Tennis were home to as many as 10,000 textile workers and textiles from across North Africa were exported in large quantities to the Eastern Mediterranean and Europe. Interestingly, historical and archaeological evidence also shows that textile exchange may have occurred between north and sub-Saharan Africa. In particular, 11th-century woolen cloth from Mali bears geometric patterns that recall northern Berber designs.

TEXTILES TODAY

Despite a growing trend toward mechanized commercial production, traditional hand-woven cloth remains important; today, a lively industry is flourishing in both exported and domestic textiles.

Throughout the region weaving techniques vary greatly in sophistication, from the simple metal framework used by the Bedouin of the Nile delta to incredibly complex devices used to weave the intricately patterned silks of towns such as Fez in Morocco.

Modern patterns often incorporate motifs designed to protect against the "evil eye," a form of harmful envy that may be directed

A Berber woman uses the traditional method of hand-spinning to turn wool into yarn ready for weaving. In her left hand, she holds the a stick, or distaff; the wool is drawn out from this onto a spindle. On her lap is a finished rug, which the Berbers are famous for manufacturing.

Rugs for sale in the narrow streets of the kasbah in the Moroccan city of Marrakech display a great variety of colors and designs. In areas where weaving occurs, each village has its own distinctive patterns.

either consciously or unconsciously by a living person. In North Africa a common way of countering the evil eye is through use of the number five or patterns incorporating five elements, such as the five-fingered shape of an outspread hand (known as the *khamsa*). Textiles with such designs are thought to protect the wearer from harm, so they are commonly used in key ceremonies, such as initiation and marriage, at which the wearer might attract others' envy. Textiles can also be highly prized gifts, and across the region the groom is often obliged to purchase fine clothes for his bride. Such gifts display the status of both the bride and the groom, and demonstrate the ability of the groom to provide for his new wife.

SEE ALSO: *Arabs; Berbers; Nuba.*

MOROCCAN RUGS

Among the most widely known North African textiles are the pile and flat weave rugs developed in Morocco. Making use of bold and colorful geometric designs, these rugs were developed during the 19th century and their popularity has turned them into a highly valuable commodity. Moroccan rugs were originally as long as 50 feet (15 m), although shorter versions are now being produced to suit the tastes of Western consumers. Designs can generally be divided into two main categories, urban and regional, with urban rugs being made in cities such as Rabat and Mediouna and various regional weaves coming from the Marrakech area and the Berbers of the Atlas mountains. Urban weaves tend to have more symmetrical designs with large medallions and borders while regional designs focus on stripes, repeating motifs, and lattices.

Any of the words printed in SMALL CAPITAL LETTERS can be looked up in this glossary.

adobe Dried clay or mud widely used as a building material throughout Africa.

age-grades The different social level in certain societies. Each person is part of an "age-set" (a group of similar-aged peers) who as they grow older move up through the various age-grades, gaining in status.

agriculturalist A settled (sedentary) farmer who makes his or her living by cultivating crops.

Allah The Islamic name for God. Like Christianity and Judaism, Islam is a monotheistic religion (that is, it has only one God).

amsar A fortress built in lands under Muslim control in medieval times, in which troops were garrisoned.

amydaz A poet or storyteller among the Berber people.

Anglo-Egyptian Condominium The combined British and Egyptian government that ruled the Sudan from 1899 (after the defeat of the Mahdist state) until independence in 1956.

bridewealth A common practice among African peoples, in which a marriage is sealed by a gift given by the groom to the family of the bride. This gift is often in the form of cattle, but may also be other livestock or money. Bridewealth compensates the bride's family for her loss.

caliph (Arabic: "successor") A political and spiritual leader of the Muslim people.

calligraphy In Islam, the art form of creating elaborate, decorative scripts of religious texts. Calligraphy is the principal art form in Islam, which forbids the representation of humans and other living beings.

caravan A group of desert traders or pilgrims, usually mounted on camels.

cataract A stretch of water on a river that is unnavigable or dangerous because of waterfalls and rapids. There are six named cataracts on the Nile River between Aswan in Egypt and Khartoum in Sudan.

clan A social group made up of several extended families or LINEAGES. Clan members often trace their descent from a common ancestor.

djinn In Islamic folklore an evil spirit.

fantasia A pageant performed by some North African peoples, most notably Berbers, which involves displays of skilled horsemanship.

Gnawa A Muslim brotherhood made up of descendants of West African slaves who were brought to the MAGHREB during the trans-Saharan slave trade. The Gnawa are renowned for their storytelling and musical skills.

hajj The annual pilgrimage to the holy city of Mecca in Saudi Arabia to pray at Islam's holiest shrine, the Kaaba, and undertake other religious duties. It is one of the Five Pillars (essential holy duties) of Islam, and so long as a person has the means to do so, she or he is expected to undertake the journey at least once during their life.

haram (Arabic: "sacred," "forbidden") In Islamic society, something that is TABOO. The "harim" or "harem" is an area of the house where women are hidden from public view.

hieroglyphs Picture symbols representing concepts, objects, or sounds. Writing systems based on these symbols were used in both ancient Egypt and Nubia.

hijab The practice laid down in Islamic law that people (both men and women) should dress modestly. The term is also used to describe the shawl or veil women use to cover their hair.

imam An Islamic religious official, who leads the congregation in prayer and addresses them on social and religious matters.

Janjaweed In Sudan, the government-sponsored armed militas, mainly composed of Baggara nomadic herders. Since 2003 they have been involved in atrocities against the settled population of farmers in the western province of Darfur.

jihad (Arabic: "struggle") In Islam, the struggle a person undertakes to submit to Allah. It may involve armed struggle, and so is often translated as "holy war." Some Muslim authorities see it as a sixth "pillar," or basic duty of Islam.

jizya In Medieval times, a poll (per person) tax levied by Islamic rulers on their non-Islamic subjects (Christians and Jews) in return for allowing them to practice their own faith.

kasbah (Arabic: "fortress") A walled citadel that provided defense for cities in North Africa.

khamsa (Arabic: "five") A hand-shaped symbol widely adopted as a good-luck charm in North Africa. It symbolizes the Five Pillars of Islam.

ksar A fortified village in North Africa.

kuth Nature spirits revered by the Nuer people of Sudan, who make offerings of livestock to them.

lineage An extended family group that shares a common ancestor. If the society traces its origins to a male ancestor and descent is traced from father to son, the lineage is termed patrilineal. If the ancestor is female and descent traced from mother to daughter, the lineage is called matrilineal.

lotar A lute used in North African traditional music.

madrasah A college devoted to the teaching of Islamic studies.

Maghreb The coastal region of North Africa, covering the modern states of Morocco, Algeria, Libya, and Tunisia.

Mahdi (Arabic: "guided one") In Islam, a holy messiah, or liberator. The Sudanese ruler Muhammad Ahmed (1844–85) adopted the title when he proclaimed a JIHAD against British occupation of his country in 1881.

Mamluke (or Mamluk, Mameluke) Originally slaves from the Caucasus and Central Asia used as warriors by the Ayyubid rulers of Egypt. They overthrew their masters in 1249 and ruled Egypt until the early 16th century.

medina (Arabic: "town") The ancient center of a city in North Africa.

minaret A slender tower attached to a mosque, from which calls to prayer are sung five times each day by a public crier known as a muezzin.

mosque An Islamic place of worship.

moussem A Moroccan festival, of either a religious or nonreligious (secular) nature.

nomad (adj. nomadic) A person who follows a wandering lifestyle, usually living by either by herding livestock or trading. The movements of nomads, such as the Bedouin or Tuareg of the Sahara, are determined by the need to find new grazing pastures, or by trade demands.

omodiya In Baggara society, a LINEAGE that claims descent from a single paternal ancestor.

papyrus (plural: papyri) A reedlike water plant. Growing extensively in the Nile Valley, it was used by the ancient Egyptians to make writing material.

pastoralist A person who lives by herding livestock such as cattle or sheep, often as part of a nomadic or seminomadic life.

People of the Book (Arabic *ahl al-Kitab*) A term in Islam denoting Christians, Muslims, and Jews, namely people who have received divine scriptures and believe in the One God (God, Allah, or Jehovah).

polygyny The practice of marrying more than one wife.

Qasidah (Arabic: "ode") The form of Islamic lyric poetry that developed in Medieval Spain under Islamic rule (Al-Andalus).

Quran The holy book of the Islamic faith. It consists of verses (*surahs*) and is regarded by Muslims as a direct transcription of the Word of ALLAH recited to the prophet Muhammad by the angel Jibril (Gabriel).

rabab (or rebab) A one-stringed fiddle used in North African traditional music.

raï (Arabic: "point of view") A very popular modern musical form in Algeria and Morocco. It is often used to protest poor social and political conditions.

raks sharki The art of so-called "belly-dancing."

Ramadan The ninth month of the Islamic calendar, held holy by Muslims as the month during which ALLAH called Muhammad to be His Prophet. Muslims fast between sunrise and sunset during Ramadan. The end of the month is marked by a major celebration known as Eid ul-Fitr.

reth A ruler of the Shilluk people of southern Sudan. All *reth* are beleived by the Shilluk to be the incarnation of their legendary first king, Nyikang.

rite of passage A ceremony, such as initiation into adulthood or marriage, that marks the passage of a person from one stage of life to another.

scarification The practice of adorning the body or face by making shallow cuts in the skin, which heal to form permanent scars. Scarification is associated in many cultures with initiation rituals marking a person's transition from childhood to adulthood. Scarification is infrequently practiced today.

Sephardim (adj: Sephardic) Jews who were expelled from Spain after the Christian reconquest of the country by the rulers of the kingdoms of Castile and Aragon in 1492. Jews had enjoyed freedom of worship and residence in Islamic Spain.

shaduf An ancient apparatus, comprising a bucket on a counterweighted horizontal beam suspended from an upright pole, used to lift water from the Nile River for irrigation.

shantytown An area of impermanent housing, usually made from scrap materials, on the outskirts of large cities where poor migrants to urban areas live. Shantytowns often lack running water, drainage, and other basic amenities.

Sharia (Arabic: "divine law") Islamic law. Sharia is based both on the edicts established by the prophet Muhammad in the QURAN and on the practices that Muhammad observed during his lifetime, which later Islamic scholars formulated as guidelines regulating the lives of Muslims.

sheikh An Islamic chief.

sirah (Arabic: "life") An oral tale, recounted by a storyteller, of the life and exploits of a famous hero figure, who may either be mythical or a real historical character.

situle A distinctively shaped copper vessel, with a tall spout and a handle, that is used to carry water by Berber women in the Atlas mountains of Morocco.

souk A marketplace in a North African city.

subsistence farming A type of agriculture in which all the crops grown are eaten by the farmer and his or her family, leaving nothing to sell for profit ("cash crops") at market.

Sufism A branch of Islam whose followers, known as Sufis or dervishes, follow a path of strict self-discipline and devote themselves to prayer in an attempt to know ALLAH directly through mystical experience. Some dervish sects are known for their trance-like circular dances.

Sunni One of the two principal branches of Islam (the other is Shia). It is made up of people who believe in the legitimacy of the first four CALIPHS who followed the Prophet Muhammad as the leaders of Islam. Shiites believe that only descendants of the Prophet's grandson Ali are rightful leaders. Sunni Muslims make up the great majority of the Islamic community worldwide.

taboo A restriction or prohibition, established by convention in a culture, which prevents a person from acting in ways regarded as inappropriate. Many taboos relate to tasks that must not be undertaken by one sex or the other, food that must not be eaten, or certain forms of clothing that may not be worn. In Islam, the term for taboo is HARAM.

tadelact An ocher-colored wall pigment made from lime and widely used on traditional buildings in Morocco.

urbanization The process by which a rural area becomes more built-up and industrialized.

wattle-and-daub A building technique that uses clay or adobe plastered on a latticework made of sticks.

yeeth (singular: yath) Divine powers in the religion of the Dinka people.

zellige Traditional Moroccan glazed ceramic tiles. Zellige are used for decorating walls or floors with brightly colored geometric patterns.

General books:

Beckwith, C., and Fisher, A. *African Ceremonies* (Harry N. Abrams, Inc., New York, NY, 2002).

Hynson, C. *Exploration of Africa* (Barrons Juveniles, Hauppauge, NY, 1998).

Mitchell, P. J. *African Connections: Archaeological Perspectives on Africa and the Wider World* (AltaMira Press, Walnut Creek, CA, 2005).

Morris, P., Barrett, A., Murray, A., and Smits van Oyen, M. *Wild Africa* (BBC, London, UK, 2001).

Murray, J. *Africa: Cultural Atlas for Young People* (Facts On File, New York, NY, 2003).

Philips, T. (ed.) *Africa: The Art of a Continent* (Prestel, Munich, Germany, 1995).

Rasmussen, R. K. *Modern African Political Leaders* (Facts On File, New York, NY, 1998).

Reader, J. *Africa: A Biography of the Continent* (Penguin, New York, NY, 1998).

Sheehan, S. *Great African Kingdoms* (Raintree/Steck-Vaughn, Austin, TX, 1998).

Stuart, C., and Stuart, T. *Africa—A Natural History* (Swan Hill Press, Shrewsbury, UK, 1995).

Temko, F. *Traditional Crafts from Africa* (Lerner Publishing, Minneapolis, MN, 1996).

The Diagram Group *Encyclopedia of African Peoples* (Facts On File, New York, NY, 2000).

The Diagram Group *Encyclopedia of African Nations and Civilizations* (Facts On File, New York, NY, 2003).

Thomas, V. M. *Lest We Forget: The Passage from Africa to Slavery and Emancipation* (Crown Publishers, New York, NY, 1997).

Books specific to this volume:

Brett, M., and Fentress, E. *The Berbers* (Blackwells, Oxford, UK, 1996).

Glasse, C., and Smith, H. (eds.) *New Encylopedia of Islam* (AltaMira Press, Walnut Creek, CA, 2003).

Harris, G. *Ancient Egypt: Cultural Atlas for Young People* (Facts On File, New York, NY, 2003).

Maxwell, G. *Lords of the Atlas* (Eland Books, London, UK, 2004).

Porch, D. *The Conquest of the Sahara* (Oxford University Press, Oxford, UK, 1986).

Rumford, J. *Traveling Man: The Journey of Ibn Battuta 1325–1354* (Houghton Mifflin, Boston, MA, 2001).

Shaw, I. (ed.), *The Oxford History of Ancient Egypt*, (Oxford University Press, Oxford, UK, 2000).

The Diagram Group *History of North Africa* (Facts On File, New York, NY, 2003).

Useful Web sites:

afrika.no/index/Countries/Egypt//index.html
Norwegian Council for Africa's resources on modern Egypt.

www.copticchurch.net
Web site of the Coptic Orthodox Church.

www.crisisgroup.org/home/index.cfm?id=3060&l=1
Campaign group for the humanitarian crisis in Sudan's Darfur region.

www.egyptologyonline.com/about_us.htm
Resources for studying Ancient Egypt.

www.nubianet.org/
Resources for the study of ancient Nubia.

www.roape.org/www_maghreb.html
Resources for the study of the Maghreb (mostly politics and human rights).

www.sudanupdate.org
Online resources for Sudan's recent history and politics.

www.uea.ac.uk/sahara/welcome.html
Current research into the Sahara and its peoples.

www.wsahara.net
Web site on the independence struggle in Western Sahara.

Bold entries in this index denote a main topic in the book. Page numbers in ***bold italic*** type indicate a major, usually illustrated, treatment of a subject. Page numbers in *italic* denote illustrations. Page numbers in brackets indicate a box feature.

A

Aaroubi 52
Aatabou, Najat 80
Ababda 36
Abbasid caliphate 21, 31, 42, 66, 68
Abboud, General 18
Abd Allah 34
Abdelaziz, Mohamed 27
Abu Simbel 61, 90
Adawayah, Ahmed 80, 82
Afro-Asiatic language family *13*, 24, 38
Agadir (33)
age-grades (86), 95
Aghlabid dynasty 31, 66
Ahaidous 54
Ahmad, al-Khalil bin 21
Ahouach 54
AIDS *see* HIV/AIDS
Aït Benhaddou 30, *33*
Aït Hadiddou 61
Al Aghlab 66
Al-Azhar University (28), *29*
Al-Hijra 60
Al-Jil 80, 83
al-Qaeda 19, 69, 70
Alexander the Great 14
Alexandria 14, *16*, 44, 50, 66, 71
Alfonso VIII 82
Algeria 4, 5, 7, 9, 13, 15, 18, 19, *26*
Algiers 16, 17, 32
Almohad empire 15, 38, 66
Almoravid empire 15, 38, 66
Amar, Abdellatif Ben 78
Amer, Ghada 46
amydaz 80
Andalus, al- (Andalusia) 25, 52, 82
Anei (Shilluk king) 102
Anglo-Egyptian Condominium 17, 34, 36, 64, 66, 84, 88, 102
Anthony, St. 50, 51
Arab-Israeli conflict 19, 22, 24, 71
Arabic language 13, 20–3, 24, 28, 29, 34, 36, 39, (43), 50, 84, 97
Arabs 12, ***24–9***, 31, 38, 45, 50, 66, 88
classic Arab music 52–3, 80
slave trade 56
Sudanese civil war 5
Aramaic 43
architecture ***30–3***
adobe 39, *89*
Berber (39)
calligraphy 42, *43*
Moroccan 100, *101*
troglodyte dwellings 32
Aririt 37
art, contemporary ***46–9***

Ashura 60
Aswan High Dam 7, 9, 18, 88, (90)
Aswani, Alaa al 23
Athanasius, St. 44
Atlan, Françoise 52, 54
Atlas Mountains 7, 9, 38, *39*, 40, 54, 61, 100, *101*
Atong 96
Augustine of Hippo, St. 38, 44
Axum, kingdom of 89
Ayyubid dynasty *15*

B

Baba-Ahmed, Rachid 83
Baggara 10, 26, ***34–5***, (65), 75, 84, 87
Baghdad 66
Bahr al Ghazal River 92
Baker, Samuel 92
Bali, Othmane (40)
Bantu 84
Banu Hillai 38, 66
Baraket, Henry 78
Baybars I 96, 97
Bedouin 15, 18, 24, 27–8, 34, 66, 75, 83, *104*
oral literature 96–7, 98
textiles 106
Beja 13, ***36–7***
Belanda (100)
Belghoul, Farida 63
Belkahia, Farid 10, 46
Ben Bella, Ahmed 18
Benhadj, Rachid 79
Beni Amir 36
Berber language 13, 19
Berbers 9, 10, 11, 12, 13, 14, 15, 19, 24, 25, 27, 29, ***38–41***, 45, 53, 66–7, 71, 72, 74, 75
dance and music 53, 54, 80, 83
Imichil bride fair (61)
metalwork 76, 77
oral literature 80, 97, 98
Spain 38
textiles *106*, 107
Beur literature (63)
Bilyana *44*
biomes ***8–9***
blood money (35)
Bongo (100)
Boudjedra, Rachid 62, 63
Boughedir, Ferid 79
Bouhadana, Albert 52, 54
Boumedienne, Houari 18
Bouzid, Nouri 79
bow harp 80
Brahem, Anouar 80
Brass 40, 76, 77
bridewealth 37, 58, 61, 75, 94
British colonies 17–18, 24, 26, 34, 36, 56, 64, 84, 88, 92, 95, 103
Bulla Regia 32
Byzantine empire 31, 45, 50, 88, 106

C

Cairo 15, 24, 28, 29, 30, 31, 48, 61, (67), 69, 77, 78
Genizah (Jewish archive) (70)

caliphs 66, 68
calligraphy 10, *20*, ***42–3***, 100, 106
camels 10, *25*, 28, (37), 61
Camus, Albert 62
Canary Islands *11*
Carthage 12, 14, 31, 45, 66, 71, 76, 79
carving 40, 100, *101*
see also sculpture
Casablanca 19, 47
cattle 28, 34, 35, 56, (58), 75
Dinka (58)
Nuer (94)
censorship 104–5
ceramics 10, (32), 40, 99, 100
Chaabi 80, 83
Chad 5, 19, 34–5, 64–5
Chad, Lake 17, 34
Chahine, Youssef 78
Charfi, Fatma 46, 49
Chérif, Mohammed 23
Cherkaoui, Ahmed 48
Choukri, Mohammed 20, 23
Chraibi, Driss 62, 63
Christianity 13, 14–15, 24, 36, ***44–5***, 56, 59, 66–8, 84, 87, 88, 92, 95, 102
Coptic Church 13, 19, 29, 50–1, 54, 60, 61, 68, 106
monasticism *45*, 50, (51), 60, 88
Monophysite doctrine 50
Constantine 44
Constantinople 50
Contemporary Art Group 48
copper 10, 76, 77
Coptic Church 13, 19, 29, 44–5, *44*, 50–1, 54, 60, 61, 68, 106
Coptic language 13, 50, 51, 54
Copts 19, 29, ***50–1***, 60, 61, 68
textiles 106
Córdoba 82
cotton 106
Council of Chalcedon 50
crafts 10, 72–3
Cushitic languages 13, 36
Cyrenaica 7, 14–15, 16, 17, 18, 28, 71
Cyrene 31, 66
Cyril, St. 44

D

Damascus 66, 68
dance and song 11, ***52–5***, 58, ***84–5***
darbouka 82
Darfur 5, 15, 16, 17, 19, 24, 34, 35, 64–5
Deir-al-Baramus 51
Deng, Francis Mading 96, 98
Derkaoui, Mustapha 78, 79
derbela 98
desert 4, 6, 8
desertification 8
Dib, Mohammed 62, 63
Dinka 10, 13, 17, 19, 34, 54, ***56–9***, 77, 92, 94
folktales and song 96, (98)
Nuer-Dinka conflict (95)
Diocletian 61

distaff *106*
Djebar, Assia 62, 63
Djerba *70*
djinn 54
Djurdjura Mountains 97
doumbek 82

E

Edict of Milan 14
Egypt 4, *105*
ancient Egyptian civilization *5*, 6, 12, 14, 31, 38, 50, 51, 54, *81*, 82, 99, 106
Eid ul-Adha 60, 69
Eid ul-Fitr 40, 60, 68, 69
Eid ul-Kebir 40, 69
ergs 6
Eritrea 36–7
Ethiopia
Axumite 89
Falasha Jews 70, 71
Nuer 92–5
evil eye 35, 41, 77, 106–7

F

Fadela, Chaba 83
Fafiti Yor (Shilluk king) 102
Fakhir, Ymane 46
Falasha Jews 70, 71
fantasias 73
Farah, Khalil 80
Farouk (Egyptian king) 18
Fatimid caliphate 15, 24, 50, 66, 67
Fatmi, Mounir 46
Feraoun, Mouloud 62, 63
Ferhati, Jilali 78, 79
festivals and ceremonies ***60–1***
Fez *32*, 54, 61, 72, 73, (82), 97, 106
Fezzan 6–7, 17, 18
French colonies 16, 17–18, 21, 22, 24, 26, 38, 62–3
French language 13, 20, 22, 62–3
French North Africa 17
funerals
Bongo grave sculptures (100)
Nubian bed burial 90
Fur 16, ***64–5***

G

Gamaa al-Islamiya 19, 69
Garang, John 19, 56, 84, 92
Ghana empire 38
Gharnati 83
GIA (Groupe Islamique Armée) 63, 69, 104
Gizeh *5*, *14*, 30, 31, 99
glass blowing (47)
Gnawa 80, 98
gold 76
Greek Orthodox Church 45
Greeks 12, 14, 31, 43, 106
Guanches (11)
guimbri 80

H

Hadandowa 37
Hafez, Abd el-Halim 52
Hafez, Khaled *48*
Haissawa *52*
Hakim 80

Hakim, al- 50
Hakim, Tawfiq al- 20, 22, *78*
Hamar 84
Hamayouni Decree 50
hammadas 8
Hasni, Cheb 83
Hassan, Fathi 46
Hassaniya 25
Hausa 72
Haykal, Muhammad Husayn 20, 21
Hebrew 13
Heiban *84–5*
Hilali 15, 24, 25
Hippo Regius 45
HIV/AIDS 74
hookah 96–7
Houdaybi, Wafaa el- (73)
hunter-gatherers 14
Hussein, Taha 20, 21, 22

I

Ibn al-Bawwab 42
Ibn al-Wahid, Muhammad 43
Ibn Battuta 15, 21, 38
Ibn Khaldun 21
Ibn Muqlah, Abu Ali Muhammad 42
Ibn Sulayman al-Muhsini, Muhammad 43
Ibrahim Pasha 84
Idris al-Sanusi 18
Idris, Yusuf 11, 23
Idrisid emirs 68
Ifriqiya 31
Imazighen 38
Imilchil bride fair (61)
Irifiyen 40
iron 10, 76
irrigation 90
Islam 5, 10, 12, 15, 16, 24, 28–9, 31, 38, 54–5, ***66–9***, 72, 84, 87, 88
calligraphy 10, 42–3, 100, 106
festivals 60–1, 68–9
Five Pillars 41, 66, 68
fundamentalism 5, 18, 19, 26–7, 44, 50, 63, 66, (69), 74
hijab 75
Kharijite 38
Khatmayah sect 37
Sharia law 37, 44, 45, 56, 64, 69, (81), 84, 90, 92, 102, 105
Shia 66, 67, 68
Spain 10, 11, 15, 25
Sufism 12–13, 36, 37, 49, 54, 55, 83
Sunni 12, 24, 34, 35, 60, 67
women 29, 41, (49), 54, 68, 75, 105
Ismail (Egyptian ruler) 17
Israel 19, 22, 24, 71
Italian colonies 17, 18, 32
ivory 89, 99

J

Janjaweed 5, 34, 35
Jazairia, Warda Al- 52
Jebel Marra 64
Jebel Si 64
Jebelein 102

Jelloun, Tahar Ben 62, 63
jewelry 10, 40, *41*, 77
Jews 13, 19, 66–7, *70–1*
  Genizah archive (70)
  Mizrahim 71
  Sephardim 52, (54), 71
jok 59
Juhayna 15, 24, 25, 34
Juok 103

K
Kababish 84
Kabyles 13, 29, 38, 96, 97
Kabylia 40, 80
Kairouan *30*, (31), 66, 68
kamenjah 82
Kammoun, Sadika (47)
Kanem-Borno 65
Karim, Mohammed 78
Karnak 99
Karoma 80
kasbah *101*, *106–7*
Kerma 14, 88
Khaled, Cheb 80, *83*
Khalifa 34
khamsa (41), 107
Khartoum 7, *17*, 37, 94
Khartoum School 48
Khatibi, Abdelkebir 62, 63
Khatmayah sect 37
Koalib 84
Koraïchi, Rachid 46, 49, (76)
Kordofan 15, 34, 84
Korongo 84
ksars 32–3, *33*
Kufic 42, 76
kujur 61
Kulthum, Umm 52, (53)
Kush 12, 88, 89
Kwango Dak Pudiet 102, *103*
Kwoth 94

L
Laabi, Abdellatif 62, 63
Lakhdar-Hamina,
  Mohamed 79
Lamdaghri, Al-Thami 52
Le Corbusier 32
leatherwork *72–3*
  Morocco leather 72
leopard-skin priest 94
Leptis Magna *30*, 31
Libya 4, *6–7*, 9, 14, 18, 71
literature
  Arabic 11, *20–3*
  Beur (63)
  French language 11, 20,
    22, *62–3*
  oral *96–8*
lotar 80
Luo 102

M
Maghreb 10, 11, 12, 13,
  15, 25, 26, 31, 45, 68,
  80, 82, 98
Mahdi, al- 34, 66
Mahdi, Salah el- 52
Mahdists 17, 34, 36, 56,
  64, 66, 84, 88
Mahfouz, Naguib 11, 20,
  (22), *78*
Mahieddine, Baya 46, 48–9
Maimonides, Moses 71
Mali 106
malouf 11, 52

Mami, Cheb 80, 83
Mamlukes 15, *16*, 24, 42–3,
  45, 67, 88, 96, 97
Mark, St. 44, 50
Marrakech *10–11*, *40–1*,
  72, 79, 98, *106–7*
marriage and the family
  74–5
masks
  Nuba *85*
Matiaat 37
Matmata 32
matrilineal societies 75, 86,
  90
Mauretania 14, 25
Mauritania 19, 25, 38
Mazif, Sid Ali 78
Mecca 24, 35, 36, 66, 68
Medina 24, 66
Mediouna 107
Mehmet Ali *17*, 36
Mernissi, Fatema 20, 23
Meroë 14–15, 88, 89, 90
Merowe Dam 88
Messiriya *35*
metalwork 10, *76–7*, 99
Milhun 52
Mimouni, Rachid 62, 63
Miri 84, 87
Mohammed Ali 64
monasticism 45, 50, (51),
  60, 88
montane grassland 9
Moors (25), 31
Moro 84
Morocco 4, 7, 9, *10–11*, 13,
  18, 26, *32*, 33, *39*, *40–1*,
  72–3
Mosteghanemi, Ahlam 20, 23
moussems 54, 61
movies 61, *78–9*
Muawiyah 68
Muhammad, Prophet 15,
  24, 42, 66
Musa, Hassan 46, 48
Musad, Raouf 20, 23
music and musical
  instruments 11, *80–3*
  oral literature 96, 97
  song 52–5, 58
  tindé 40
  World Sacred Music
    Festival (82)
Muslim Brotherhood 18, 69
Muslim Sisters 29
Mzabi 38

N
Napata 88
Napoleon Bonaparte *16*, 21
Naskh 42
Nass El-Ghiwane 80
Nasser, Gamal Abdel 18,
  19, 52, 53, 69, 71
Nasser, Lake 7, 18, (90), *91*
Nastaliq 42
Ngungdeng 95
Nhialic 59
Nile Delta 7, 9, 106
Nile River 4, 6, 7, 8, 12,
  14, 18, 27, 90, 92, *93*
Nilesat (105)
Nilo-Saharan language
  family 13, 34, 56, 64, 84
Nilotic peoples 13, 56, 88,
  92, 102

Nimeri, Colonel 36
nomadic peoples 4, 13,
  24–6, 84
  Baggara 35, (65), 84
  Bedouin 15, *25*, 27–8,
    96–7, 98, *104*, 106
  Beja 36–7
Nourredine, Cheikh 80
Nuba 10, 13, *84–7*
Nuba Mountains 84, 87
Nubia 7, 12, 14–15, 16, 18,
  24, 25, 31, 34, 45, 61, (89)
Nubians *88–91*
Nuer 10, 13, 17, 56, 59, 61,
  75, 77, *92–5*, 98
  Dinka-Nuer conflict (95)
  ghost marriage (75)
Numidian kingdoms 14, 38
Nyala 64
Nyikang 102, 103

O
oases 6, 8, *9*, 40
oil reserves 87
omodiya (35)
Open Studio Project (48)
Oran 83
Otoro 84
Ottoman empire 16, 17, 24,
  50
Ouargla 82
Ouarzazate 32–3
oud 82

P
Pachomius, St. 50, 51
patrilineal societies 75, 86
Persians 12, 14, 21
Pharaonic Race 61
Phoenicians 14, 31, *43*, 76
Picasso, Pablo 47
poetry 52–3, 80
  Arabic 11, *20*, (21), 97
Polisario Front 19, 27
polygyny 35, 37, 68, 75, 86
population statistics 4, 74
Port Sudan 36

Q
Qaddafi, Muammar *5*, 18, *46*
qanun 82
qasidah 11, *21*, 52, 97
Quran 10, *21*, 24, 35, 42, 73
Qutb, Sayyid 69

R
rabab 80, 82
Rabat *30*, 32, 107
Rachedi, Ahmed 78, 79
Raï 80, *83*
rainmaking ceremonies 61,
  84–5, 87
raks sharki 82
Ramadam 68
Rami, Ahmed 53
refugees *5*, *19*, 36, 64, 92
Reggab, Mohamed 79
religion
  rites-of-passage 58, *59*,
    61, (86), 94, 95
  sacrificial offerings 58,
    59, 60, 61, 69, 94, 103
  spirit possession 95
  see also Christianity;
    Coptic Church; Islam
Rio de Oro 27

Riqa 42
rite-of-passage ceremonies
  58, *59*, 61, (86), 94, 95
rock art 10, 14, 46
Roman empire 12, 14–15, 31,
  38, 44, 45, 50–1, 66, 71
Rosti, Stephan 78

S
Saadawi, Nawal el- 20, 22,
  23
Sadat, Anwar el- *5*, 19
Sahara *6–7*, 8, 10, 12, 14,
  15, 27–8, 34, *37*, 38
Sahel 6, *37*, 38
Saladin (Salah ud-Din) 15,
  31, 67
Sanaa 52
scarification 61, 90, *95*
"Scramble for Africa" *4*, 17
sculpture *99–101*
Sedira, Zineb 46, 49
Sefrioui, Ahmed 11, 62–3
Selim, Ali 48
Senac, Jean 62
Sennar 88
Sephardic song 52, (54)
Septimus Severus 38
Shaabi 11, 80, 82, 83
shaduf 90
Shaeri, Hamid el- 80
Shallagea 37
Sharawi, Hoda 29
Shenouda III (Coptic Pope
  and Patriarch) 50, 51
Shilluk 13, 94, *102–3*
  coronations (103)
Shuwa Arabs 34
Sidi Mohammed El Merheni
  61
silver 40, *41*, 76, 77
Sinai Desert *25*, 45, 66, *104*
Sirat al-Sultan Baybars 96, 97
Sirry, Gazbiah 46, 48
Six-Day War 19, 24, 71, 82
slavery and the slave trade
  Arab traders 56
  Gnawa 98
  Mamlukes 15
  Nubia 89
  Nuer 92
  Sudan 17, 34, 56
Smail, Paul 63
souks 10, *11*
Spain
  Islamic 10, 11, 15, 25,
    38, 52, 66, 82
  Sephardic Jews (54), 71
  Spanish colonies 11, 16,
    17, 19, 26, 27
Spanish Sahara 27
Sphinx 14, *99*
spindle *106*
SPLA (Sudanese People's
  Liberation Army) 19, 56,
  81, 84, 86, 92, 102
Sudan *5*, 12, 18
Suez Canal 17, 18
Sulaym 15, 24, 25
Surur, Naguib 20, 22

T
taarija 82
tadelact (32)
Takfir wal Hijra 69
Taliq 42

Tama 34
Tamasheq 13, 38
Tarifit 38
Tassili N'Ajer 14
Tel el-Kebir, Battle of *17*
television and radio *104–5*
Telouet *101*
Tennis 106
textiles 10, *11*, 40, *49*,
  106–7
  carpets and rugs 10, *39*,
    40, 106, *106–7*, (107)
Theodosius I (Roman
  emperor) 44
Thuluth 42, *43*
Tibesti Mountains 6
Tigre 36
tindé (40)
Tira 84
Tlili, Mustapha 62, 63
To-Bedawiye 13, 36
tourism 4, 10, 19, 32
trade
  Britain *16*
  Jews 70, 71
  slave trade *see* slavery
    and the slave trade
  trans-Saharan 6, *11*, 15,
    17, 38, 40, 98
Triki, Gouider 10, 46
Tripoli 17, 72
Tripolitania 7, 15, 16, 17,
  18, 25
troglodyte dwellings 32
Tuareg 10, 13, 77
Tullishi 84
Tunisia 4, 7, 9, 13, 14, 18,
  19, 73
Tutankhamun 106

U
Umayyad caliphate 31, 66,
  68, 81
Uqba ibn Nafi 31
Urabi Pasha 17
urbanization 4, 27, 33

V
Vandals 45
vegetation 8–9

W
Wa 59
Waddai sultanate 34
wadis 6, 8
Wahaab, Mohammed abd
  el- 52
Western Sahara 19, (27),
  28, 104
whirling dervishes 54, *55*
White Nile 9, *93*
wool *106*
written language 11, 20, *21*,
  42–3, 96

X, Y, Z
Yacine, Kateb 62, *63*
Yaqut al-Musta'simi 42
yeeth 59
Zahounia, Chaba 80
Zar cult 90
Zawahiri, Ayman al- 69
zellige (32)
Zidane, Zinedine 38
Zirhan, Emil 54
Zubair, al- 34